LIFE SKILLS FOR TEENS

How to Cook, Clean, Manage Money, Fix Your Car, Perform First Aid, and Just About Everything in Between

By
KAREN HARRIS

ISBN: 978-1-951806-40-8

TABLE OF CONTENTS

INTRODUCTION

Congratulations, you are a teenager! The big question is, now what? The teenage years are an exciting yet ever-changing period of your life. New challenges and tasks seem to pop up almost daily--not to mention all the transitions your body is going through.

As you get older and take on more responsibilities, you have probably wondered how to do many of the adult tasks your parents or older siblings seem to breeze through daily. Everyday challenges like how to tell if the chicken in the fridge has gone bad to how to get rid of dandruff have likely crossed your mind. As you learn and experience new things, questions about basic life skills will arise. This book is here to help you solve the daily problems adults take for granted.

While the internet provides a wealth of knowledge, it can be overwhelming to navigate at times. I mean, which of the thirteen articles about budgeting and saving money is actually accurate? And yes, you can ask your parents or other trusted adults in your life to teach you specific skills, but sometimes you just want to figure it out on your own. That's where this guide comes into play.

In the following pages, you will learn the ins and outs of many everyday tasks, problems, how-tos, and recommended guidance needed for entering adulthood. This guide breaks down tasks into easy-to-digest, step-by-step instructions with illustrations to help.

Need to know how to write a check or choose the best health insurance? No problem, we've got your back. Are you confused about what all those numbers and percentages mean on your box of cereal? It's all explained in this book. And, when you're ready to host your first party, we'll help you successfully pull off your gathering—from the guest list down to what goes on the invitation.

This guide is organized into easy-to-navigate chapters and sections so that you can quickly find the information you need. In addition, the labeled illustrations and diagrams break many tasks down even further, providing a visual compass to more fully explain the crucial details of each how-to.

While we know a book can't answer all of life's questions, we can certainly try to cover the main ones that are likely to pop up as you venture out on your own. So, whether you're simply looking to become more independent, getting ready to head to college, or moving out on your own, our Life Skills for Teens Guide has all the essential information you need to make a successful start.

If you're ready to embrace your teen and young adult years with a self-reliant attitude, dive in and learn how to accomplish your first independent skill!

SECTION ONE:

FOOD & KITCHEN

1. Eating Healthy

Making smart decisions for your health begins with the foods you put into your body. While junk food is always at our fingertips, healthy teens know how to balance the junk with the good stuff, even when your mom is not peering over your shoulder.

There used to be a food pyramid as a visual guide, but now there is the food plate.

HEALTHY EATING PLATE

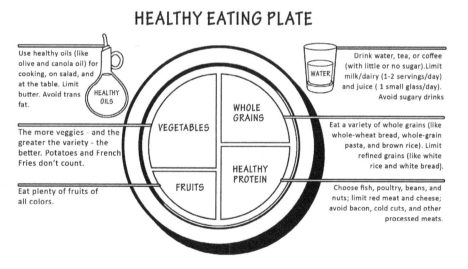

Use healthy oils (like olive and canola oil) for cooking, on salad, and at the table. Limit butter. Avoid trans fat.

HEALTHY OILS

The more veggies - and the greater the variety - the better. Potatoes and French Fries don't count.

Eat plenty of fruits of all colors.

VEGETABLES

FRUITS

WHOLE GRAINS

HEALTHY PROTEIN

WATER

Drink water, tea, or coffee (with little or no sugar).Limit milk/dairy (1-2 servings/day) and juice (1 small glass/day). Avoid sugary drinks

Eat a variety of whole grains (like whole-wheat bread, whole-grain pasta, and brown rice). Limit refined grains (like white rice and white bread).

Choose fish, poultry, beans, and nuts; limit red meat and cheese; avoid bacon, cold cuts, and other processed meats.

Finding the right daily balance of fruits, vegetables, grains, proteins, and fats is crucial when making healthy choices.

The majority of what you should eat is fruits and vegetables. These can be fresh or frozen, but avoid canned because of the high levels of sodium.

An excellent way for a teen to get more fruits and vegetables in their diet is by making smoothies - you can also get some protein by using milk or Greek yogurt.

GRAIN ANATOMY

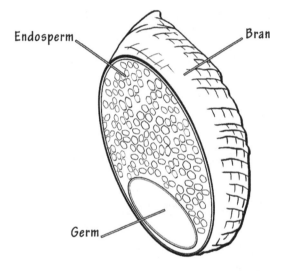

Other areas to focus on are whole grains and lean proteins. Whole grains are products that use the entire grain seed instead of a seed that is broken down.

You may already enjoy some healthy whole-grain foods like popcorn, oatmeal, brown rice or bread, and crackers made from whole wheat.

Lean proteins build your muscles, including foods such as chicken breast, turkey breast, tuna canned in water, eggs, tofu, white fish,

Greek yogurt, cottage cheese, lean beef, beans, powdered peanut butter, and shrimp.

One essential part of staying healthy is drinking plenty of water. Some people take stock in the eight glasses a day, but there is no proven number; just be sure to stay hydrated all day long. Purchasing a fun water bottle that fits your personality can be one way to stay motivated.

Lastly, limit the amount of oils, fats, and sugars you consume. The human body needs these to function, so don't completely cut them out; just make them the smallest part of your diet. After all, everyone wants to indulge in sweets from time to time.

2. Picking Out Produce

Learning to select produce properly will help you get all the fruits and veggies you need into your diet. Unfortunately, there is no cut-and-dry answer across the board, so we'll cover some general rules as well as how to pick out some popular plant-based choices.

Avoid Brown Spots

When soft brown spots begin to appear, that means produce is passing its peak freshness and should be eaten ASAP. While one little brown spot on a peach or apple will not harm you, there is no reason to bring that fruit home from the store, especially if no one will be eating it immediately.

If you notice a piece of fruit with a brown spot, simply use a small knife to cut it away, and the rest should taste just fine.

The one exception is bananas; a banana that is beginning to brown will taste sweeter. The brown spots indicate the banana's starch is turning into sugar, so browned bananas are ideal for baking and smoothies!

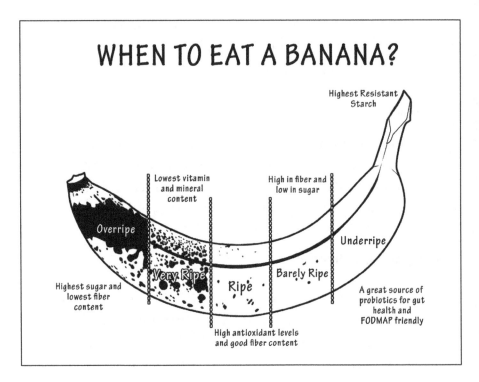

WHEN TO EAT A BANANA?

Highest Resistant Starch

Lowest vitamin and mineral content

High in fiber and low in sugar

Overripe

Underripe

Highest sugar and lowest fiber content

Very Ripe

Ripe

Barely Ripe

A great source of probiotics for gut health and FODMAP friendly

High antioxidant levels and good fiber content

Avoid Limp Vegetables

Vegetables should look crisp, firm, and fresh. If they are beginning to feel soft, spongy, or drooping, they are not the vegetables for you. Greens such as spinach, lettuce, and arugula can go bad very quickly; make sure the leaves look crisp and bright before selecting them for your next salad. Greens that start to rot will develop a green sludge in the container.

Selecting Melons

The best way to tell if a melon is ripe is to smell it. Both cantaloupe and honeydew should emit a fragrant smell from the point where the vine was attached. Think of it as the melon's belly button!

You should inspect the melon for any soft spots as these are an indication the melon could be rotting inside. Give the melon a few taps; if it sounds hollow, it is ripe and fresh.

Picking Berries

When selecting berries, look at the container's underside to see if any berries have been smashed or are beginning to mold. Since berries are so soft, it is easy for them to become damaged in transit. Take a few moments to inspect all around before placing them in your cart.

When in doubt with produce, one general rule of thumb is that it is probably going bad if it is soft. Some fruits, such as peaches, plums, avocados, oranges, and pears, should have some give to them. However, when you gently push on them, and it causes a bruise or a break in the skin, it is past its peak freshness.

3. How to Read a Food Label

The Food and Drug Administration (FDA) is the government entity that oversees food labeling and ensures food companies are honest with their customers.

Per the FDA, all food labels in the USA must contain the name of the food, the quantity in the container, nutrition information, allergen information, and the manufacturer and distributor's name and address.

There are even font size and type requirements to ensure food labels are uniform and easy for consumers to read. With all of this information, the next question is, what does it all mean?

NEW LABEL/ WHAT'S DIFFERENT

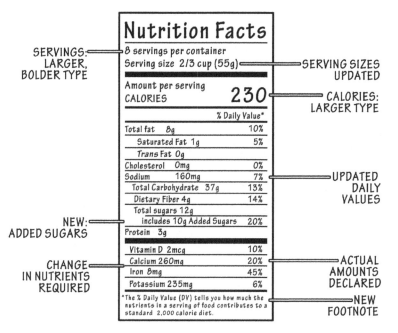

SERVINGS: LARGER, BOLDER TYPE

Nutrition Facts

8 servings per container
Serving size 2/3 cup (55g)

SERVING SIZES UPDATED

Amount per serving
CALORIES **230**

CALORIES: LARGER TYPE

% Daily Value*

Total fat 8g	10%
Saturated Fat 1g	5%
Trans Fat 0g	
Cholesterol 0mg	0%
Sodium 160mg	7%
Total Carbohydrate 37g	13%
Dietary Fiber 4g	14%
Total sugars 12g	
includes 10g Added Sugars	20%
Protein 3g	

NEW: ADDED SUGARS

UPDATED DAILY VALUES

Vitamin D 2mcg	10%
Calcium 260mg	20%
Iron 8mg	45%
Potassium 235mg	6%

CHANGE IN NUTRIENTS REQUIRED

ACTUAL AMOUNTS DECLARED

*The % Daily Value (DV) tells you how much the nutrients in a serving of food contributes to a standard 2,000 calorie diet.

NEW FOOTNOTE

At the top of the label, the serving size is listed. It is advised to pay attention to the serving size because most containers have several servings.

The nutrition information listed will be for ONLY ONE SERVING, not the entire box or bag.

The left-hand side will outline the amount of each nutrient, vitamin, sugar, fat, etc., while the right-hand side will show you the daily percentage for that category.

All percentages are based on a 2,000-calorie diet for an adult. For example, if a yogurt container says it contains 15g of protein, it equals 30%; this means the average adult has met 30% of their protein quota for the day after eating the yogurt.

```
Nutrition Facts
Serving Size 1 Tub (150g)

Amount per serving
Calories    90                  Fat Cal 0
                              % Daily Value
Total fat 0g                        0%
  Saturated Fat 0g                  0%
  Trans Fat 0g
Cholesterol  <5mg                   1%
Sodium  60mg                        3%
Potassium  210mg                    6%
Total Carbohydrate 7g               2%
  Dietary Fiber 0g                  0%
  Sugars 5g
Protein 15g                        30%
Vitamin A 0%    •    Vitamin C 0%
Calcium  15%    •    Iron      0%
```

These numbers and percentages can help people who are attempting to maintain a balanced and nutritional diet.

4. Meal Planning and Shopping for Healthy Food

One of the best ways to ensure that you eat a healthy and well-balanced meal is meal prepping. There are three styles of meal prepping.

- ❑ Batch Cooking - cooking large quantities of dishes like chili, soup, or a casserole and eating that for dinner or lunch each day of the week or freezing half to use in a few weeks.
- ❑ Individual Meals - cooking all the components to a meal and placing each portion in a separate container, so it's easy to grab and go or reheat. Think of it like a freshly made frozen dinner.
- ❑ Ingredient Prepping - preparing large quantities of ingredients you frequently use when cooking, such as

slicing peppers and onions, mixing salad dressings, or roasting and slicing up a chicken to be used in various meals.

All three styles require planning, but they also save money. When consumers make frequent trips to the grocery store, they end up spending more!

To decide what to eat, determine what you like or what you'd like to try, and follow the healthy food plate recommendations. A well-balanced meal will have lean protein, whole grain, and fruits and vegetables. Use oils such as extra virgin olive oil or avocado oil to cook instead of butter.

To properly meal prep and plan, you will need suitable containers to keep food fresh!

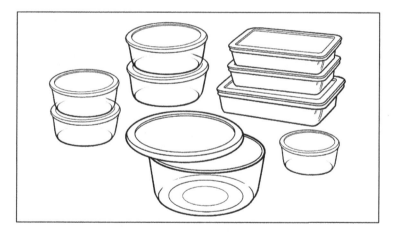

If meal prepping is not for you, consider going to the grocery store twice a week to purchase fresh ingredients. It is helpful to keep your kitchen stocked with commonly used items such as spices, salt, pepper, cooking oil, rice, beans, quinoa, whole-wheat pasta, tomato paste, chicken broth or bouillon cubes, vinegar, eggs, flour, honey, milk, and plain Greek yogurt.

The more you cook, the more you will know what you commonly use and need to keep on hand.

5. Proper Food Storage

Once you bring home all your delicious and healthy foods to cook, you will need to store them properly to prevent them from spoiling or going stale. Of course, all food will "go bad" at some point but knowing the best way to store it will provide optimal freshness for as long as possible.

Many foods require refrigeration, or they will spoil and develop harmful bacteria. Meat, fish, eggs, dairy, juices, and some fruits and vegetables require refrigeration.

- Fruits that require refrigeration: berries, cherries, grapes, citrus, melons, and avocados (only after they are ripe).
- Vegetables that require refrigeration: broccoli, cauliflower, celery, leafy greens, green beans, mushrooms, carrots, beets, and radishes.

Potatoes, onions, and winter squashes should be stored in a cool, dark place. Tomatoes, avocados (before ripening), apples, bananas, eggplants, and peppers can be stored at room temperature.

Perishable food will have a "use by" or "best by" date on their packaging. It is crucial that you follow the guidelines and discard any food that is past the "use by" date. If the "best by" date has passed, the food may still be okay to eat.

FOOD STORAGE: EXPIRATION DATES

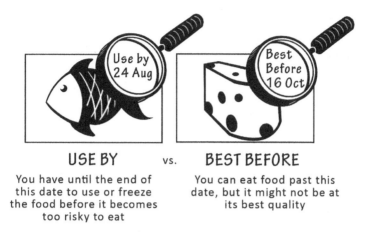

USE BY	vs.	**BEST BEFORE**
You have until the end of this date to use or freeze the food before it becomes too risky to eat		You can eat food past this date, but it might not be at its best quality

If food smells or looks funny, be on the safe side and discard it.

By looking at or smelling meat, you can often tell rather quickly that it has gone bad. However, here are some basic guidelines for determining if your meat is still good to eat.

Beef: If the meat has changed color from a bright red to pink to a dull brown or gray, it is spoiled.

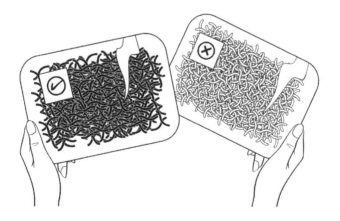

Chicken: Healthy chicken has a natural gloss and a slight odor to it. Spoiled chicken will emit a strong smell, be slimy or sticky, and change color from fresh and pinkish to dull and gray.

Fish: Fish has a naturally strong odor, so if it smells "fishy," that is NOT an indication it has gone bad. Fish is typically white or pink, so if its flesh begins to turn blue, gray, or take on a milky-white appearance, it is spoiled. Spoiled salmon will also start developing spots.

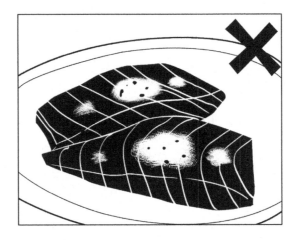

Grain products like cereal, pasta, rice, crackers, etc., aren't likely to spoil, but they will lose their freshness and become stale, soft, and mushy if not stored properly. You should store opened grain products in air-tight containers to maximize their shelf life.

Grains and flours also have the potential to attract flour mites. These are tiny bugs that love to live in your opened grains. While the mites themselves are not typically harmful, they can cause other foods to spoil or mold as they spread bacteria.

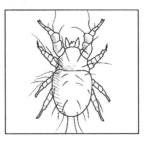

Flour mites are pale and small and nearly impossible to see. If your grains or flour emit a minty smell, you likely have mites.

Flour weevils are larger, brown, and easier to spot.

In both cases, dispose of the grains and do a thorough search through your dry goods as it is likely they have spread to other unsealed grain products.

You will need to thoroughly clean your pantry and cabinets to ensure they are all gone. You can look for a food-safe pesticide to use, or you can use a bleach and water solution.

Both cloves and bay leaves are natural deterrents to weevils, so placing them in your pantry and even in your dried food containers can help prevent contamination.

Bread and pastries do have the ability to develop mold, so check those products for signs of decay if you are unsure of how fresh they are.

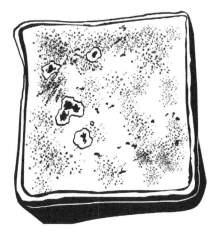

6. Kitchen Tools

Now that you know what to do to make healthy meals, you need to learn how to use various kitchen tools!

- Measuring Tools

When baking, it is essential to follow measurements precisely, whereas cooking allows for a little more leeway depending on taste.

The most common measuring tools used in the kitchen are measuring spoons and measuring cups for dry and liquid ingredients.

Measuring spoons usually range from ⅛ teaspoon to 1 tablespoon, while measuring cups typically range from ¼ cup to 1 cup. The measurements need to be level at the top unless the recipe specifically calls for a "heaping" amount.

Liquid measuring cups are different than dry measuring cups in that they look like a tiny pitcher. You will get a more accurate liquid measurement if you use the correct type of cup.

- Whisk and Spatula

Two essential kitchen tools are the whisk and the spatula. A whisk blends and adds air to the ingredients by using a swift swirling motion, known as "whisking." A spatula is a flat utensil used for blending and folding ingredients into each other as well as scraping down the sides of a bowl. A silicone spatula is excellent to use with non-stick pans as it won't scratch the surface.

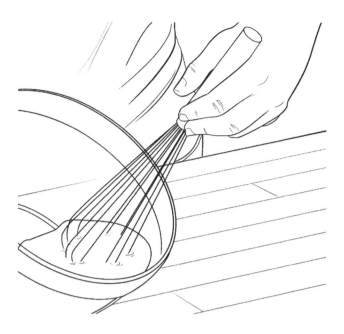

- Grater and Zester

A grater is a sharp, four-sided (usually) tool used to grate fresh cheese, vegetable shavings, and fruit skins. A zester finely shreds the skin of citrus fruits.

- Kitchen Knives

There are different types of knives for different types of cutting.

❑ A bread knife is serrated or looks like it has teeth and is used to cut bread loaves.

❑ A chef knife can cut most things and is excellent for raw meat, fruits, and vegetables.

❑ A paring knife is small and is an excellent tool for cutting the tips of fruits and vegetables or peeling and cutting up smaller fruit.

❑ A slicing knife looks like a smaller version of a bread knife and is suitable for cutting cooked meats.

I didn't cover every type of knife, but I have included a helpful diagram.

KNOW your KNIVES

	Chef Knife
	Sontoku Knife
	Bread Knife
	Filleting Knife
	Boning Knife
	Carving Fork
	Cleaver Knife
	Slicing Knife
	Vegetable Knife
	Paring Knife
	Peeling Knife

- Cutting Board

A cutting board is an essential tool if you do not want to ruin your countertops. It would be best to have a separate cutting board for meats, fruits, and vegetables, so cross-contamination does not occur.

Raw meat carries the risk of Salmonella, Escherichia coli (E. coli), Shigella, and Staphylococcus aureus, resulting in food poisoning and even death. Cooking the meat to the proper temperature kills these bacteria.

- Meat Thermometer

It is wise to use a meat thermometer to avoid eating undercooked meat and fish. Each type of meat has a recommended internal temperature. An electric thermometer is best, so you do not have to worry about misreading it.

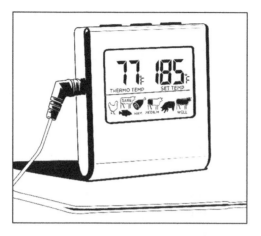

When using a meat thermometer, the temperature stick's pointed end needs to be inserted into the middle of the meat's thickest portion to receive the most accurate temperature.

- Pots and Pans

There are various kinds of pots and pans you will use when cooking. As a starting chef, you should become familiar with a skillet, a pot, and a baking pan.

❑ A skillet is a pan with a raised lip used on the stovetop to cook meat and vegetables. Non-stick skillets are great because you don't need to use very much oil to keep the food from sticking to the bottom, but the non-stick coating can wear off or become damaged.

❑ A pot has high sides and is used on the stovetop for cooking broth, soups, noodles, and sauces.

❑ A baking pan is used inside the oven for cooking various dishes such as casseroles, lasagna, cakes, or roasted meats and vegetables.

Skillets, pots, and pans come in several shapes and sizes but start with a 10" skillet, 4-quart pot, and 9x11 baking dish.

7. Kitchen Appliances

The kitchen is full of gadgets and appliances that can seem complicated and overwhelming if you do not know how to use them. Those used for cooking are the oven, stovetop, microwave, toaster, and toaster oven.

- Oven - An oven is used for baking or roasting food. To properly use an oven, you need to set it to the correct temperature. All ovens are different; some have a dial, and some are digital. Average cooking temperatures range from 350-450° Fahrenheit. The recipe, or the prepackaged food, you are preparing will tell you at what temperature to set the oven.
- Wait until the oven has preheated to the desired temperature before putting the food inside. You will need to set a timer to ensure the food you are cooking doesn't burn. Again, some oven timers are digital, and some older ones have a dial setting. You can also use a separate kitchen timer that sits on the counter.
- Stovetop - Most modern homes have an oven/stovetop combination; however, there are instances where the oven and stovetop are separate appliances. The stovetop is used for cooking, sautéing, simmering, and boiling. Burners can be electric or gas and set at various temperatures from low to high.

  If you have a gas stovetop, the pilot light must stay lit, or you will be at risk for carbon monoxide poisoning. But don't stress; they rarely go out on their own. If you smell gas in your home, check the knobs to ensure they were not accidentally turned on or that the pilot light is out. When you twist the knob of a gas stove, you will hear a clicking sound; if the flame doesn't light, try again. Typically, you need to push the knob in and twist at the same time.

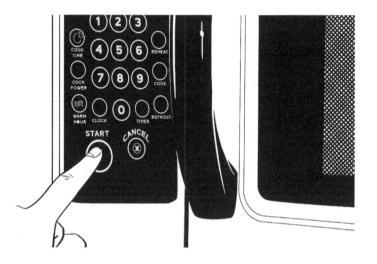

- Microwave - The microwave is relatively easy to use and navigate. It is perfect for reheating items or cooking frozen meals. If you cook something prepackaged or canned, there should be instructions on how long to heat the item. Typically, you push the corresponding numbers on the keypad and hit start. So, if something says to heat for two minutes, you would press 2:00 and START. Pretty easy!

The one caveat is that microwaves come in different wattages. The wattage of a microwave range from 1200-6000 watts. The higher the wattage, the stronger the microwave. The directions may vary depending on the wattage.

NEVER put anything metal into a microwave, including aluminum foil, foil take-out containers, or utensils, as it can cause sparks and possibly a fire.

- Toaster - A toaster is probably the easiest kitchen appliance to use. Toasters are used to toast bread, bagels, English muffins, etc. While toasters have a heat setting, typically on a dial, unless you like your things very dark or very light, leaving your toaster on the number three setting is effective for toasting most items to a nice golden brown.

  Some toasters have a bagel button; since bagels and English muffins are thicker, pushing this button will add a little time to ensure proper toasting.

- Toaster Oven - A toaster oven is like a mini oven. It is an excellent tool for a teen to use because it doesn't require you to heat the entire oven to make a small meal or snack, which saves energy. Toaster ovens work like their larger counterparts: set the temperature, allow it to warm up, place the food inside, and set the timer. Cooking times for toaster ovens should be about the same as if you were using a regular oven.

8. Washing Dishes

Everyone's mother, grandmother, uncle, and cousin have their own way of washing and drying dishes properly, so if someone has taught you a method that seems to work - then there is no reason to read this section. However, if you find yourself out on your own for the first time and have a sink full of dirty dishes but no idea how to clean them properly, this is the section for you!

Start by scraping off all the food left on the plates or bowls.

Next, fill your sink with hot soapy water. Take one dish at a time and scrub it clean. You can use a dish brush or sponge. If you use a sponge to clean your dishes, the sponge needs to be disinfected or replaced regularly to prevent bacteria from forming.

❑ Ways to clean a sponge:

- 2 tablespoons of bleach and 4 cups of water. Soak the sponge for 5 minutes, then rinse with water.
- Soak the sponge in water and microwave on high for 1-2 minutes.
- Put the sponge in your dishwasher and use the setting for heated drying.
- Soak your sponge in vinegar for 5 minutes and rinse.

After you wash your dishes, rinse them off with clean, hot water. Place them on a drying rack to air dry, or dry with a clean towel.

Once you are done, clean your sink! Leave sponges and brushes to air dry. Once a sponge starts to show wear and tear, throw it away.

SECTION TWO:

PERSONAL GROOMING

1. Maintaining Hygiene

Keeping your body healthy and clean is an important responsibility you take on as a teen. While your parents may have bathed you in your youth, it is time for you to take control of your hygiene as a teen.

As the human body grows into adolescence, it begins to smell. Sorry, but it is true. Children as young as eight should be using deodorant. The older you get, the more pungent the body odor.

Body odor develops because of hormone production. Hormones make our sweat glands produce more sweat in the underarm and groin area, and when the bacteria breaks the sweat down, *voila* - we start to smell.

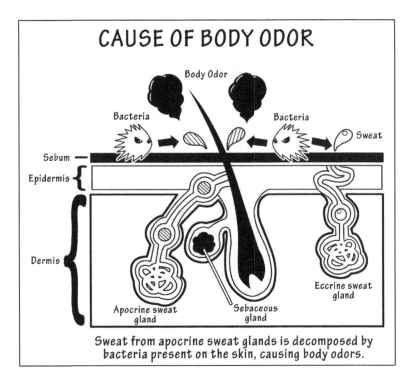

CAUSE OF BODY ODOR

Body Odor

Bacteria

Bacteria

Sweat

Sebum

Epidermis

Dermis

Apocrine sweat gland

Sebaceous gland

Eccrine sweat gland

Sweat from apocrine sweat glands is decomposed by bacteria present on the skin, causing body odors.

The good news is that there is plenty we can do to prevent and combat body odor. The first and probably most important is bathing.

There is much debate over whether or not you should bathe every day. Some people say yes, while others say it is not good for your skin.

It will also depend on your activity level and the weather. If you were outside on a warm spring day playing ultimate frisbee with your friends for two hours, you probably need a shower; whereas if it was 20° outside and you stayed bundled up reading books, you can probably take a pass that day.

In addition to bathing, brushing your teeth, wearing deodorant, clipping/filing your fingernails and toenails, and regularly washing your hands are all ways to keep your body and odor in check.

Keeping your hands and nails clean is one of the best things you can do to keep yourself healthy as well. Germs love to hide under nails, and they breed in the warm, moist environment there.

If you have long nails or keep them painted, it is even more important to wash your nails properly, as bacteria can also grow in the cracks and chips that develop in polish. Consider using a nail brush to make sure you rid yourself of all the germs!

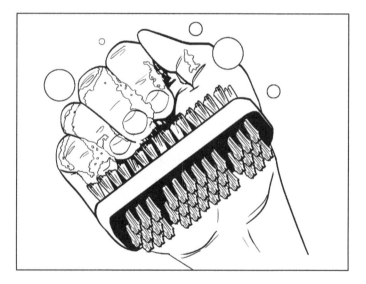

2. Shaving

Both boys and girls typically have hair on their bodies they wish to shave. Boys will usually shave their facial hair, and girls generally, choose to shave their legs and underarms.

❑ Shaving Your Face

- Before you begin shaving your facial hair, it's important to hydrate your face. Hydrating will help prevent nicks and cuts. You can use an exfoliating scrub or moisturizing face wash.
- Next, lather shaving cream on your face on the areas you need to shave.
- Check your razor and make sure it is not dull. A dull razor will lead to cuts. A disposable razor will last roughly 5-10 shaves.
- Use light and gentle strokes and apply light force to the razor. You can go both with and against the grain. Do what feels the most comfortable.
- Once you are finished, wash your face with cool water and use moisturizer or aftershave.

❑ **Shaving Legs & Underarms**

- Before you are ready to shave your legs and underarms, make sure they are hydrated. Usually, women shave in the shower, so spend a few minutes washing your hair or body to give your pores time to open.
- Exfoliating first is also helpful to avoid nicks and cuts.
- Lather your legs with shaving cream and apply gentle pressure as you use long steady strokes.
- For underarms, repeat the above step but use small strokes.
- Use a sharp razor and be gentle around the knees and ankles, as these areas can nick easily.
- Once you finish, rinse off the shaving cream or gel and apply moisturizer.

3. Taking Care of Your Skin

Good skincare often leads to a healthy body. Our skin provides an outside layer of protection for our bodies. Exfoliating, washing, and moisturizing your skin are three steps you can take to ensure your skin keeps its healthy glow.

Different people will find various products they prefer to use; sometimes, it takes trial and error to figure out what you like best. Some people will have allergic reactions to specific products, so you may wish to perform a skin test before using any new products if you have a history of allergies.

SKIN PATCH TEST

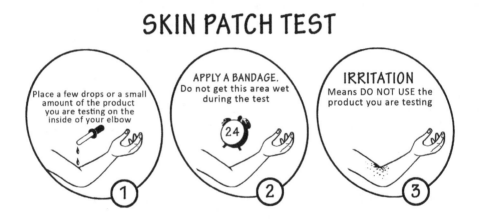

Boys and girls can benefit from developing a skincare routine, both morning and night.

Another proven way to keep your skin healthy is to stay hydrated. Our skin is 64% water, so drinking plenty of water each day will keep your skin healthy.

WATER IN HUMAN ORGANS

ORGAN	%WATER
Skin	64
Skeleton (bones)	31
Muscle	79
Brain	73
Liver	71
Heart	73
Lungs	83
Kidneys	79

Sugary drinks like soda and juice are fine in moderation, but your main beverage should be water as you go about your day.

4. Feminine Hygiene

Women and adolescent girls have additional hygiene practices that need to be followed because females experience menstruation.

Menstruation occurs when the female body sheds the thick lining of the uterus the body has prepared in case a fertilized egg is implanted.

In general, when a female is experiencing menstruation, the body produces additional odors. There are specific washes and cleaning wipes available to balance the pH of the female body.

Regular bathing, using these specialized products, and regularly changing your tampon or menstrual pad will help keep those odors at bay.

Never insert deodorants or other scented products inside the vagina, as they can cause allergic reactions and mess with your body's natural pH.

5. Healthy Hair

If our hair is not healthy, it will turn brittle, crack, and break off. Longer hair runs the risk of becoming damaged because some people will stop cutting it to maintain its length and keep it growing. While your hair will likely grow long, it will be unhealthy.

Healthy hair needs to be trimmed regularly, every three to four months, to keep it growing and strong. Regular trims prevent breakage, flyaways, and split ends, as well as keeping your hair shiny, sleek, and healthy.

If your goal is to grow long hair, mention that to your stylist, and they can do a very minimal trim. That way, your hair stays healthy, and you don't lose any length.

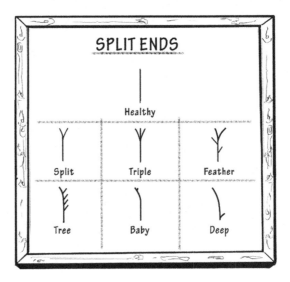

Some signs that you may be due for a trim include:

- Visible split ends
- Ends that break off or snap easily
- If your hair appears to be thinning out
- Hair that appears to have stopped growing - your hair IS growing, but because it is damaged, the ends keep breaking off or splitting.

Keeping your hair healthy also means maintaining a healthy and itch-free scalp. Some people will never suffer from dandruff or an itchy scalp, but many will. One out of five people will experience dandruff at some point, and men are more likely than women to have dandruff.

Dandruff is caused by seborrheic dermatitis, a common skin condition that can also affect skin areas around the ears, eyebrows, nose, back, and chest.

Over-the-counter products typically work well to solve this itchy and sometimes embarrassing problem. The trick, dermatologists say, is finding a product in which the active ingredient is sulfur-based — for example, zinc or tar.

Itchy scalp is different from dandruff and can be caused by weather conditions and stress.

Adding a few drops of tea tree oil or coconut oil to your shampoo or conditioner is one way to help alleviate a dry and itchy scalp.

TEA TREE OIL for
ITCHY SCALP

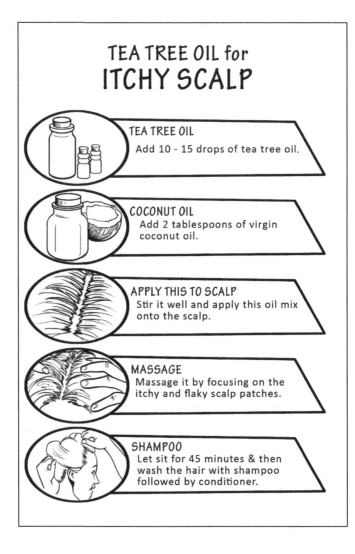

TEA TREE OIL
Add 10 - 15 drops of tea tree oil.

COCONUT OIL
Add 2 tablespoons of virgin coconut oil.

APPLY THIS TO SCALP
Stir it well and apply this oil mix onto the scalp.

MASSAGE
Massage it by focusing on the itchy and flaky scalp patches.

SHAMPOO
Let sit for 45 minutes & then wash the hair with shampoo followed by conditioner.

SECTION THREE:

PERSONAL HEALTH

This section contains information on first aid and basic health conditions. This information is in no way intended as medical advice, nor should it be taken as such. You should always consult a doctor when you have questions or concerns about your medical care, treatment, and symptoms.

1. Basic First Aid

Once you become a teen, taking care of your cuts and scrapes is a beneficial skill. While there is nothing like a mother's touch, first aid is a skill that has many applications throughout life.

- Cuts

If you cut yourself, immediately apply pressure to the wound. You may need stitches if the bleeding soaks through the bandages and doesn't stop in 5-10 minutes while applying pressure.

Assuming you don't need stitches, once the bleeding has stopped, wash the cut with warm water and soap and apply a bandage.

- Minor Burns

Cover a minor burn with a cool, moist bandage or wet cloth, or hold the burn area under cold water. DO NOT APPLY ICE. Once the burn has cooled, apply a gel such as aloe vera or a moisturizer and wrap it loosely with a clean bandage.

- Sprained Ankle

If you suspect a sprained ankle, elevate the leg and apply ice for 20 to 30-minute intervals every two to three hours. Do this as much as possible for the first two or three days.

Keep the ankle elevated higher than your heart when lying or sitting down. Wrap your ankle with a bandage to help reduce swelling.

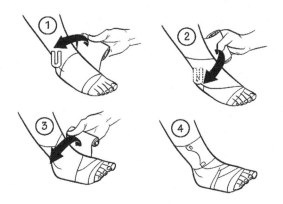

- Nosebleed

If you or someone else is experiencing a nosebleed, sit down and tilt the head forward. Pinch the nose just below the bridge, but don't pinch the nostrils closed. You can also apply ice to the bridge of the nose if bleeding is intense and doesn't seem to slow down.

- Bee Stings

As soon as possible, remove the stinger from the sting site. Apply an ice pack to reduce swelling and take an antihistamine to reduce swelling and possible itching. You can also take ibuprofen or acetaminophen to help with any pain.

If the person appears to be struggling to breathe or develops a severe rash or hives, they may be allergic to bees. Call 9-1-1 if the person stung by the bee is having difficulty breathing.

2. Keeping Yourself Healthy

You play a significant role in maintaining your health. Of course, regular exercise and a healthy diet are important, but you can do other precautionary things to maintain your health.

Wash your hands. Washing your hands correctly and regularly is one of the best sickness-prevention methods that exist.

Everything we touch has germs, so you are gathering germs on your hands every time you touch something, even if you clean and sanitize regularly.

Hand sanitizer is helpful if you do not have access to a place to wash your hands, but it does not and should not replace actual hand washing.

It is recommended that you wash your hands:

- After using the restroom (yes, even if you don't touch anything)
- Before and after eating
- Before and after preparing food
- After you have sneezed, coughed, or used a tissue
- Before and after treating a wound
- After changing a baby's diaper
- After handling pet food
- After touching an animal
- When you come home
- When you arrive at work

- After taking out the garbage or recycling
- After touching your nose, eyes, or mouth

The proper handwashing technique from the Center for Disease Control (CDC) is as follows:

- Wet your hands with clean, running water (warm or cold), turn off the tap, and apply soap.
- Lather your hands by rubbing them together with the soap. Lather the backs of your hands, between your fingers, and under your nails.
- Scrub your hands for at least 20 seconds.
- Rinse your hands well under clean, running water.
- Dry your hands using a clean towel or allow them to air dry.

Living in a post-COVID-19 world means that handwashing is more important now than ever (although it's always been pretty important). The more you can do to keep yourself healthy, the more you are doing to keep those around you healthy.

3. Common Cold & Flu Self-Care

At some point in your adult life (probably at several), you will come down with a cold and possibly the flu. Even if you get the flu shot every year, wash your hands all the time, and never touch your face, you will still get sick at some point. That is unless you become a hermit and never have contact with the outside world, which is unlikely.

The common cold and the flu are both caused by viruses, so there is no medication to cure them. A virus attacks the cells in your body and uses those cells to reproduce virus cells like themselves, which is what makes you sick.

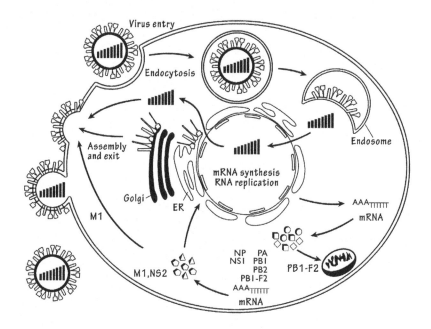

A flu vaccine usually wards off several strains of the flu virus and will likely lessen your symptoms should you catch it, but once you have a virus, it has to run its course.

While there may be no cure for a virus, there are plenty of things you can do to alleviate some of the symptoms and make yourself more comfortable.

- Hot liquids like non-caffeinated tea or chicken broth will keep you hydrated.
- Over-the-counter cold medicines to relieve symptoms of cough, congestion, and runny nose.
  - Always read all labels to make sure you take the correct dosage and don't take two medicines that shouldn't interact.

- Over-the-counter pain and fever reducers like ibuprofen and acetaminophen.
- Naps and plenty of rest.
- Use a humidifier.
- Honey to relieve a cough or sore throat.

Colds and the flu are very similar, but there are ways to help you determine whether you have one or the other. Below are the common symptoms associated with a cold and the flu, according to the CDC.

Cold Symptoms:

- sneezing
- runny or stuffy nose
- sore throat
- coughing
- postnasal drip
- watery eyes

- fever (not common)

Flu Symptoms:

- fever (not everyone with the flu will have a fever)
- cough
- body aches
- sore throat
- runny or stuffy nose
- headache
- chills
- fatigue
- diarrhea and vomiting (occasionally)

Both a cold and the flu can turn into something more serious on occasion, so it is recommended you call your doctor if:

- Your symptoms last more than ten days with no improvement.
- You have a fever lasting more than four days, or your fever is over 103°.
- You have a cough that is worsening, or you are having trouble breathing.
- You are having difficulty urinating.
- Persistent pain in the chest or abdomen.
- Severe fatigue or dizziness.
- Severe muscle pain.
- Any time you are concerned about your symptoms.

4. Scheduling a Doctor's Appointment

Until you are 18, you will not be able to see a doctor without your parent's permission. The only exception to this is if it is an emergency.

When you seek medical care on your own, you will first need to confirm whether the doctor accepts the health insurance you have. You can typically obtain this information by calling the office directly, contacting your insurance company online, or via a telephone call.

When you call to make an appointment, they will ask for your personal information, such as your name, date of birth, address, and why you are seeking an appointment. The office will likely verify your insurance information as well.

If it is your first time visiting this doctor, plan to arrive at least 15 minutes before your appointment time because you will likely have paperwork to fill out and forms to sign.

And remember, just because you are 18 now doesn't mean you *have* to go to the doctor alone. A parent can still accompany you, but it is probably time you start taking on these grown-up tasks one by one to prepare you for becoming an adult.

5. Talking to the Doctor

Taking on the responsibility of talking to the doctor on your own may seem frightening or overwhelming, but remember that doctors are there to help us and make us better!

To feel more confident when you go to the doctor alone, write a list of questions down ahead of time; that way, you won't forget what to ask if you feel nervous.

If your visit to the doctor is because of a health concern you have, write down any symptoms you've noticed. Having this list ready will make your visit run smoothly, and the doctor will be able to treat you more efficiently if they understand what is going on.

Some people prefer to see a doctor of the same gender as themselves, especially if they have something private they wish to discuss. If that is the case, make it known when you schedule your appointment so the office staff can assign you the best match for your needs.

6. Mental Health & Wellness

Taking care of your mental health is just as important as taking care of your physical health.

The CDC reports that as of 2018, 3.2% percent of children between the ages of 3-17 have depression, which equals roughly 1.9 million children and teens.

Roughly every 100 minutes, a teenager commits suicide, and suicide is the third leading cause of death in people ages 15-24.

These numbers are not included to frighten you but instead to help you understand that depression and anxiety among teens and young adults are common ailments. It is normal and OK if you feel this way and need to seek help.

Signs of depression include:

- sadness
- feelings of hopelessness
- spending more and more time alone
- losing interest in favorite activities
- feeling sluggish and tired
- talking about death or suicide
- headaches
- decreased appetite
- problems in school

If you are feeling or experiencing any of these warning signs, talk to someone. It can be a relative, trusted adult, school counselor, or friend.

If you feel like you have no one to talk to, call SAMHSA's National Helpline at 1-800-662-HELP (4357).

Fortunately, there are many things you can do to help boost your overall mental health and well-being.

Getting adequate sleep is chief among them. Teens ages 14-17 need an average of 8-10 hours of sleep a night. More often than not, teens who are stressed about school and other obligations fail to meet this amount — making sleep a priority can do wonders for your overall mental health.

Avoiding drugs and alcohol seems like a no-brainer, but the temptation is everywhere for teens and young adults. Young bodies and brains are not fully developed; in fact, the human brain does not stop developing until roughly age 25.

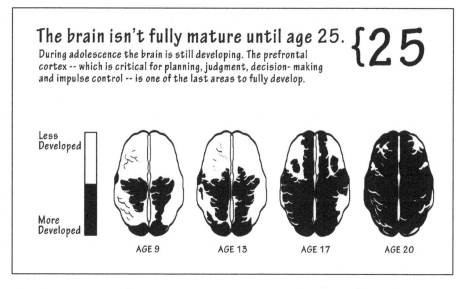

The brain isn't fully mature until age 25. {25

During adolescence the brain is still developing. The prefrontal cortex -- which is critical for planning, judgment, decision- making and impulse control -- is one of the last areas to fully develop.

Less Developed

More Developed

AGE 9   AGE 13   AGE 17   AGE 20

The final part of the human brain to develop is the prefrontal cortex, which is responsible for impulse control, critical thinking, judgment, and decision-making.

When you introduce drugs and alcohol into the mix, your developing brain struggles even more to make the right choices.

Its always hard to focus.
I'm never good enough
Terrible Headache!
I should have stayed home.
This is TOO MUCH
I'm exhausted
My grades are dropping
I'm not able to do this.

Find time to relax and spend with friends, family, or other people close to you. Our bodies and our brains need to recharge, and these days a teen's schedule can be so jammed full of activities that there is no time to slow down and breathe.

If you are struggling to manage your schedule, find a trusted adult you can talk to and discuss which activities you may be able to let go of. There is nothing wrong with saying, "This is too much for me right now."

Even if you cannot unload anything from your busy schedule, listening to your body and knowing when to take a break is essential, and it is a skill that will serve you well as an adult.

A fifteen-minute nap or meditation session can do wonders. A hot shower with loud music playing (assuming you won't annoy other people in the house) is soothing and relaxing. Sitting down and reading a book for 20 minutes can provide you with an escape.

You know yourself best and what it takes to relax and recharge; just be sure to do it once in a while and remember, there is no shame in seeking help if you believe you are struggling with a mental health condition.

7. Understanding Health Insurance

Health insurance can be a tricky thing to understand. There is no one-size-fits-all plan in the U.S. The information provided here is generic but enough to give you an understanding of what to look for and how insurance works.

No matter what type of plan you have, it is recommended that you directly contact the insurance company if you have questions about whether something is covered.

If you would like to get an idea of what something would cost, you can ask your doctor to submit a pre-authorization. A pre-authorization does not guarantee coverage, but it will give you an idea of your out-of-pocket cost. Some procedures require a pre-authorization first.

- PPO vs. HMO vs. HSA

PPO

Probably the most standard and universal healthcare plans are PPOs. PPO means Preferred Provider Organization. This type of insurance will require you to use their preferred or in-network provider to receive the best rates.

PPOs will allow you to use out-of-network doctors, but you will likely end up spending much more money. However, if you have a particular doctor you are attached to, and they do not take your insurance, you should be able to visit their office as part of your insurance plan.

HMO

An HMO or a Health Maintenance Organization requires you to be assigned to a specific doctor or practice as your primary doctor. If you require any specialized treatment, you will need a referral from your primary care provider to a specialist who accepts the insurance. If you have an HMO plan, you will not be able to see any doctor outside of the network unless you plan to pay all the costs yourself.

HSA

An HSA, also known as a Health Savings Account, is a PPO plan that allows members to set aside a specific amount of pre-taxed dollars for medical costs. These plans usually have a debit card linked to an account where the pre-tax dollars accrue until they are used. In some instances, members can use these dollars to buy medical supplies, equipment, vitamins, etc.

- Deductibles

A deductible is a set limit that the member will need to meet before certain services are covered by insurance. Some standard amounts for deductibles are $500, $1000, $1500, and $2000, although they can go much higher or lower.

After you meet the deductible, your insurance will break down what percentage of the rest of your care would be covered if you required medical treatment. For example, after the deductible is met, you may have 80% coverage, which means insurance would pay 80% of the cost, and you would be responsible for 20%.

CO - INSURANCE

Insurance Company   Subscriber

80/20

CO-INSURANCE

- Preventative Care

48

Preventative care is the care you receive from your doctor to prevent major illnesses and medical issues from happening. This type of care includes annual physicals, screenings, and immunizations.

Due to the Affordable Care Act, private insurance companies must cover preventative care services at no cost to the patient. These services are to be covered without the requirement of meeting the deductible.

- Insurance Cards

Your insurance company will issue an insurance card that details essential information about your plan. You should carry your insurance card with you at all times in case of an emergency.

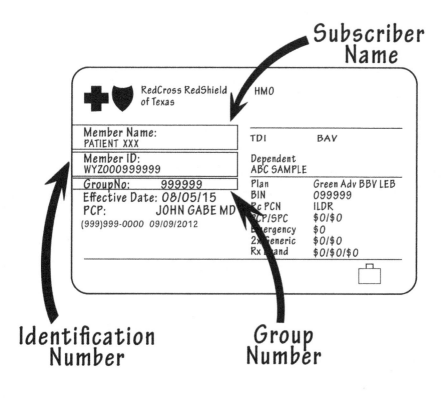

On your insurance card will be your name or the person who holds the insurance, which may be one of your parents. Other information may include:

- o Subscriber number: this is a unique number to you and anyone else in your family.
- o Group number: this number will be the same for anyone on the plan as a whole. For example, if you have your insurance through your mom's workplace, everyone who works where your mom does and has this same insurance will have the same group number.
- o If it is an HMO, it will have the name of your primary care physician.
- o It may also have a prescription drug plan number as well.
- o The back of the card will list several different phone numbers, including the number that you, as a member, would call if you had questions.

- Explanation of Benefits (EOB)

An EOB is the form you (or your parents) will receive after medical treatment has been completed and the insurance company has paid for your claim. An EOB is NOT a bill from your doctor; however, it will show what you are responsible for paying as the patient.

An EOB will list:

- Service(s) provided
- How much the physician charged
- How much the insurance company "allows" (an amount they determine based on the procedure and average price where it was performed)
- What the insurance paid

- Amount applied to the deductible
- Patient responsibility: what you are required to pay

Explanation of Benefits (EOB)- This is not a bill

Member: [ ][ ]
Member ID: [ ][ ]
Claim#: [ ]
[ ][ ]

Date of Service	Description	Cpt Code	Amount Billed	Amount Allowed	Not Covered	Co-Pay/ Co-Insurance	Deductible
☐ ☐ ☐	▭	☐	☐☐	☐☐	☐☐	☐☐	☐☐
			☐☐	☐☐	☐☐	☐☐	☐☐

PLAN PAYS: $☐☐
PATIENT RESPONSABILITY: $☐☐

If anything is not covered by your insurance, there will usually be a code provided. For example, it may read "L4" next to the item not paid. The EOB will give an explanation either at the bottom or on the back of the form.

*L4 Procedure not covered by plan or *L4 Amount applied to the deductible*

If anything on your EOB does not make sense or you believe there is an error, you have a right to call your insurance company and seek further clarification. You can also contact your doctor to make sure they billed the procedure correctly.

On occasion, doctor offices will accidentally use the wrong code or date, which could result in the denial of your claim.

Insurance is a tricky thing, no doubt, but taking time to understand the basics will serve you well as you progress through life. No one can be a better advocate for you than you!

MONEY & BUDGETING

1. Saving Money

Saving money is probably one of the most challenging but important skills you can learn. We live in a world where everything we want, from food to clothing, to gadgets to entertainment, is at the tip of our fingers. A few swipes on our phones and *voila* - in minutes, or at most a few days, the object we ordered is in our hands.

It is very tempting and easy to spend money as soon as we get it, but learning how to save will not only benefit you as an adult, it will allow you to put money aside for the items you'd like to purchase in the future.

The general rule of thumb is that you should save 20% of every paycheck. That means if you make $100 babysitting, you should put $20 into savings.

It sounds simple enough, but saving can be difficult for many people to put into practice. If you have a job where you receive a paycheck, ask for a direct deposit. You can usually arrange with your employer to put a set amount into a savings account and the rest into your checking account.

Some people find it easier to save a set amount each week or month instead of a percentage. For example, you might save $10 from every paycheck, whether you work 5 hours or 15 hours.

If setting up a direct deposit is not an option, it will be up to you to set aside some money each time you are paid.

It helps some people to visualize a goal when they have difficulty saving. Maybe you want to save up for your first car or school band trip to California, or perhaps it's a $150 pair of Nike shoes; whatever the case, picture that item when you are struggling with saving.

2. Making a Budget

One way to help you reach your monthly savings goal is to create a budget. A budget is when you estimate how much money you will have coming in and how much you can spend. Some things teens might budget for include food, clothing, gas, car payment, entertainment, and savings.

Your budget is going to be affected by what you make and what your expenses are. If you only make $100 a month, you cannot budget to spend $125.

Most teens will have a variable budget, meaning the amounts you have coming in and going out will often vary, making it difficult to know how much you have to spend. To help with this, start by listing your "must pay" expenses, such as a car payment or cell phone payment, if you have one.

Car: $50
Savings: $15
<u>**Gas: $30**</u>
TOTAL: $95

If you use the example above, you can see the first $95 each month is spoken for. Let's say you make $150 a month working part-time. Once you subtract the $95 of expenses from your $150 earnings, you will have $55 a month left over to spend as you see fit. That could mean hanging out with your friends, buying something you need, or a gift for your mom's birthday.

3. Opening a Bank Account & Using an ATM

If you are going to have a job and a paycheck, you will need to open a bank account. You must be 18 years old to open a bank account without a parent or guardian.

Each bank will have its own set of rules, but all banks will require a form of photo identification. Some banks require two. Forms of I.D. could be a driver's license, state I.D. card, or a passport. You may also be required to bring your social security card or birth certificate.

Additionally, you will need to provide your address, date of birth, phone number, and likely an email.

Lastly, you will be required to make an initial deposit; amounts vary, so ask the bank before you arrive.

Essential questions to ask before you decide on a bank:

- Do they require a minimum balance to be maintained (how much do you need to keep in the bank without being charged a fee)?
- What is their overdraft policy (what happens if you take too much money out of your account)?
- Do they charge for checks?
- Is there a monthly fee?
- Is there a fee to use an ATM not associated with the bank?

Using an ATM - ATM means Automatic Teller Machine. An ATM is where you can use your bank debit card to retrieve cash. Your card is linked directly to your bank account, so you cannot pull out more money than you have available.

When signing up for a bank account and receiving your debit card, you will create a PIN. A PIN (Personal Identification

Number) is a four-digit code you will use every time you access an ATM or use your card to make a purchase.

Make your PIN something you will remember but **DO NOT** use your birthday or a set of numbers easily associated with you, like your house number or the last four digits of your phone number.

Most ATMs will ask for your PIN immediately after you insert your card. The screen will then ask you to follow a series of prompts, including what type of transaction you are making and which account you would like to use. Some people have their savings account linked to the same debit card, and some banks allow for cash advances, which work like credit and require you to pay back what you borrow with interest.

4. Writing A Check

Writing a check may one day become obsolete, but that day hasn't arrived yet, so knowing how to do it may come in handy. For example, when renting your first apartment, most realtors or landlords expect a deposit, and the easiest way to do this is via check. Writing a check instead of using cash also provides you with an automatic receipt should there be any issues.

The process is pretty straightforward, but let's walk through it, so you understand each step.

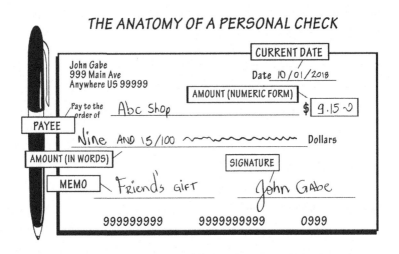

The top left corner will have your name and address. On the top right corner, you will need to write the date of the check.

The next line is where you write the name of the person or place receiving your payment. Next to the person or place receiving the check is a box to write the numerical amount, for example, $123.12.

On the line below, you will write out the amount in words. Using the amount above, it would read, "One hundred and twenty-three and 12/100. The cents portion is always written as a fraction over 100.

The bottom left is the memo section; you can use it to remember why you wrote the check. On the right-hand side is where you will sign.

If, for any reason, you make a mistake on the check, use a black pen or marker and write VOID across the front of the entire check. It is also a good idea to shred any voided checks instead of throwing them away, as it has your account information printed along the bottom.

5. Applying for a Credit Card

Credit is something most people need in life but struggle to control. Credit is necessary to buy a car, a home, and sometimes even to get a job or rent a home.

Much like opening a bank account, you will need to be 18 years old to open a credit card account, and you will need to prove to the bank or credit institution that you have the capital (salary) to make regular payments.

Most credit card companies offer starter credit cards for people who have never had credit before. These will come with a low spending threshold, as banks will want to make sure you are a responsible user before extending your credit line.

Before deciding which card to go with, research available offers: compare interest rates (the lower, the better), annual fees, late fees, and other penalties or fees you may be responsible for as the cardholder.

It may also be possible to get your first credit card by becoming an authorized user on one of your parent's accounts. If your parents are willing to do this, then it is your job to show them you deserve this level of trust and responsibility, as your credit usage will reflect on their credit score.

Over time, by making responsible choices (not maxing your card out), making your payments on time, and not opening several credit lines at once, you will start to build a credit score.

A score of 600 is average and an excellent place to start, but it's advisable to aim for the mid to high 700s. A good score is key if your plans include significant purchases like a home or car in the future.

Credit is there so consumers can extend their buying power, so while it might be ideal to pay your card off each month, don't expect that to be the norm. While paying it off each month is fantastic, at least make the minimum when you can't make the entire payment.

If you cannot pay the total off, pay as much past the minimum as you can. This habit will save you money over time and keep your credit score in good standing.

SECTION FIVE:

MAKING GOALS AND KEEPING THEM

1. Deciding on a Goal

Before you can go about setting a goal, you need to narrow down your options. Making vague statements such as, "I want to be healthier" or "I want to get better at sports" will not set you on a path to success.

Of course, you need to start with a broad idea, but it's important to narrow down the options before setting and working towards a goal.

This process starts by being realistic about any obstacles that may stand in your way. For example, if your overall goal is to be healthier, but you know that you despise running, be honest with yourself and cross running off as a way to achieve your goal. Then, think about forms of fitness you DO enjoy.

Another example would be if your goal is to read more books, but you don't have easy access to a library; you will need to look at your options to obtain other ways of accessing books.

When you are honest and list the real limitations, you open yourself to your actual possibilities. Maybe you enjoy swimming or playing tennis; perhaps you can plan a monthly trip to the library and pick up several books at once or decide to ask your friends about setting up a book exchange system.

Write down all of your options concerning setting your goal, know where you stand realistically, and then you can work towards deciding on the specifics of the actual goal.

2. Setting Reasonable and Achievable Goals

Setting a goal seems pretty straightforward, but it is surprising how many people are ineffective at setting goals. That is because we often don't know the correct way to set them.

The first step in setting a goal is to decide what your endgame is. Do you want to attend Harvard, become a motorcycle mechanic, or become the first chair violinist in your school's orchestra? Name your specific goal.

Next, you need to realize you will not achieve this in a week or a month and that it may even take years. And this is where most people fail.

To achieve a goal, you have to set smaller attainable goals along the way, keeping you motivated and heading in the right direction.

If your goal is to become the first chair violin, perhaps the first goal you set for yourself is that you will practice for one hour every day for the next four weeks.

Once you've achieved that, pat yourself on the back, give yourself a reward (like an afternoon off from practicing to see a movie!), then set the next goal. Maybe this time, you choose a complex piece of music to master, and off you go.

Experts recommend using a tool like a vision board to keep you motivated and on target.

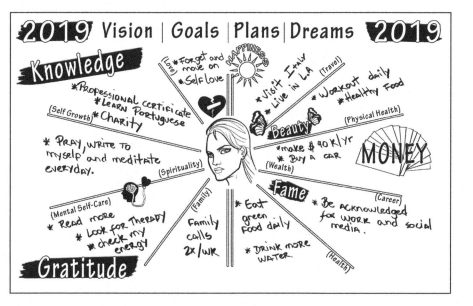

3. Resources to Achieve Your Goal

While you will be performing the lion's share of the work to achieve your goal, nobody makes it to the top alone. A crucial part of achieving your goals is knowing where to seek help and resources.

Your resources will vary based on your goal, but one excellent place to start is the public library. Public libraries and librarians are skilled in assisting patrons in accessing educational information, training, scholarships, tutors, books, and other print resources.

If you want to ace the SATs, then you may need a tutor and a reputable study guide.

Another valuable resource can be people who are already doing what you want to achieve. If you're going to be a mechanic, go talk to mechanics and perhaps even get a part-time job as one. If you want to become a better baseball player, talk to older, more seasoned players to seek advice.

Finding a mentor or tutor that can help you achieve your goal provides you with one-of-a-kind insight.

4. Handling Failure

Okay, so you didn't achieve your goal. You came up a little short, or you crashed and burned; either way, you feel lousy.

While I wish there were a magic wand to wave when we fail, to make all the bad feelings go away, life does not work that way. So, what do we do when we fail at something or suffer a major disappointment?

Well, after you have ranted and raved, ate junk food and milkshakes with your best friend, cried in your pillow, or thrown your pillow against the wall, you get back up, and you try again.

There is a quote by the ice hockey legend, Wayne Gretzky, that schools should hang in every building and every person should read. It says: *"You miss 100% of the shots you don't take."* You've probably heard it before, but it is true.

If you don't even try again, you have automatically failed.

You may realize that after you fail to meet your goal, your priorities have shifted, and that's okay. No one is saying you have to keep going after something if you have indeed changed your mind, but you shouldn't give up just because you failed.

There will be some goals you simply can't attempt again because of circumstances. For example, you spent a month practicing your audition song and then didn't get the lead in the musical. Okay, so that chance is gone, but you *can* continue to practice and learn singing, and maybe you'll get the part next time.

When you fail at something, give yourself time to grieve and then reassess your plan. What about your circumstances can you control, and what is beyond your control? Can you study more, practice more, save more money, etc.? If so, outstanding - make a new plan!

If you cannot control certain factors, then work on accepting them and putting them to the side. The quicker you learn to accept that you cannot control all aspects, the easier it will be to move forward.

When all else fails, find a new goal to focus on. Sometimes stepping away for a bit and reflecting can help us refocus on our priorities and what we wish to achieve.

5. Looking Towards the Future

Being a teen and figuring out what you want to do with the rest of your life is a daunting task, but have no fear; no one expects you to have everything figured out all at once.

If you feel bombarded by choices and options and are not entirely sure what you want career-wise, consider taking a career aptitude test. There are several free tests and questionnaires available online that might provide insight.

These tests will ask you questions about things you like to do, careers you think you may or may not enjoy, things you are skilled at, and things you do NOT want to do.

While no test can guarantee whether or not you will enjoy or succeed in a career, it may help those struggling to find a sense of direction.

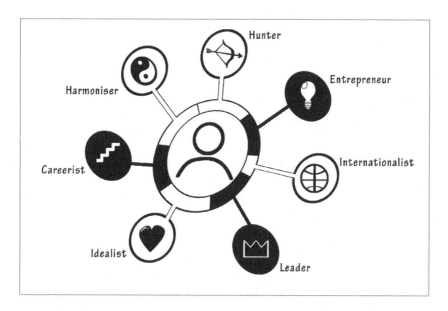

If you are still struggling or need more guidance, speaking to your school counselor or a trusted teacher may be another helpful resource.

If you have a particular interest in a specific career path, consider volunteering or asking someone in the field if you can shadow them for a day. Getting hands-on experience can often make or break a person's interest in something once they realize what is involved.

Once you decide what career path you might like to take, do as much research as possible into the education and schooling requirements, the costs associated with obtaining that education, and schools you can attend.

For example, if you dream of becoming a marine biologist, there may not be a school near your hometown, so are you willing to attend school in Florida or California?

One final note about planning for the future is that it is okay to change your mind. Many people start college undecided, change their major, or do not attend college until much later in life, if at all!

Career changes happen, and life experience can go a long way in terms of educating you.

The average person will change their career 5-7 times! Humans, by nature, are curious beings that love to learn and adapt. So have no fear if you are not entirely sure where the future leads because, in all honesty, none of us do.

SECTION SIX:

COPING WITH EMOTIONS

Dealing with strong emotions can be scary and a real struggle for some people depending on their personality and upbringing. In some families and cultures, expressing emotions is taboo. Some people may have expectations about what feelings are appropriate for men versus what is appropriate for women.

"Emotions aren't masculine or feminine. They're human. Normalize them."
- @Hii_Frenn

Learning how to name, understand, and work through your emotions is a life-long skill that will benefit you greatly through the teen and early adult years.

1. Managing Feelings

Before you can manage your feelings, you need to be able to label them. If you tend to be impulsive, this may be a challenge, but it is worth the effort. Strong emotions tend to cause knee-jerk reactions and rash decisions that we later regret.

When something happens that causes a strong emotion to wash over you, take a minute or two and breathe deeply while naming the emotion. It may be anger, jealousy, fear, disappointment, or even positive emotions like joy or excitement. Just be in the moment and feel whatever it is you need to feel before you react.

If a situation doesn't require an immediate response, such as reliving the moment when you received a grade you disagreed with, or a text that upsets you, don't jump to respond. Walk away, reflect, and come back no sooner than 30 minutes after the event.

If you need to, talk to someone outside the situation. Talking to a trusted person often provides much-needed relief and saves us from making rash decisions.

Other ways to help process strong emotions include going for a walk, listening to music, dancing, taking a hot shower or bath, journaling, and yoga.

Once you have had time to process your emotions and are no longer feeling their intensity, you are ready to revisit the situation and respond or handle it in a calm state of mind.

2. Accepting Your Emotions

As mentioned in this section's opening, some people may have difficulty accepting their emotions due to cultural or personal beliefs, so it is important to understand that ALL feelings are valid. You have the right to feel any way you want about a situation - you can even cry! Crying can be an appropriate and healthy way to express strong emotions.

One exercise to help you with accepting emotions is to visualize them. Try this the next time you have a strong feeling:

- Close your eyes and imagine yourself putting space between you and the emotion.
- Imagine what the emotion looks like: what size is it, what shape, what color?
- Once you have defined what it looks like, imagine it for a few moments sitting out there, away from you.
- When you feel ready, allow the emotion to float back inside you.
- Reflect on the experience. How did it feel to put some space between you and your emotion? Did it feel different once you allowed it back in?

3. Managing Anger & Self-Control

Anger can be a complicated emotion to control because it is also one of the scariest. Often when we feel angry, we feel out of control and not sure which way to turn.

There is a reason that anger is also associated with fire; often, when we are angry, we feel hot. Our skin flushes, and we may even begin to shake.

There is science behind this. When we are angry, our body prepares for a fight. The adrenal glands flush our body with cortisol and adrenaline, and our brain begins to push blood towards our muscles.

Since blood to our brain decreases, we also lose the ability to think critically. This reaction is called "fight or flight." Humans are hardwired this way, thanks to our ancestors, who had to decide to fight or flee when faced with life-threatening situations.

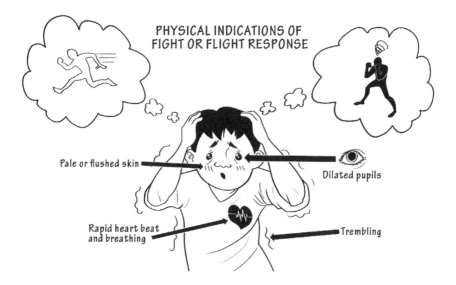

PHYSICAL INDICATIONS OF
FIGHT OR FLIGHT RESPONSE

Pale or flushed skin

Dilated pupils

Rapid heart beat
and breathing

Trembling

When angry feelings come upon us, it is crucial to slow down and take deep breaths to provide much-needed blood and oxygen to the brain.

Simple exercises that can help you calm down include counting, stretching, making and releasing fists, and walking away from the trigger.

Counting backward slowly from tengives your brain time to calm down before responding and distracts your brain from the thing that is causing you to feel distressed.

If you're feeling very angry, count to ten...

Staying physically active and engaging regularly in yoga, meditation, and mindfulness can also help you deal with anger.

73

Mindfulness and meditation can provide you with techniques and visualizations to use when you face stressful and anger-inducing situations.

BREATHE IN, BELLY OUT

- Place one hand on your chest and the other on your belly

- Inhale deeply through your nose for a count of four, making sure your belly is expanding and not your chest. Exhale for a count of four.

- Continue this breathing cycle for a few minutes.

- Feel the stress leave your body as your mind becomes calm.

When being confronted by a person who is angering you, if possible, distance yourself from the individual, walk away, go into another room, or back away.

Let the other person know why you are leaving or moving, and ask them to respect your space. Maintain an open pathway between you and the other person, so no one feels trapped. Do your best to present non-threatening body language. If needed, tell the person that you want some time to think before you continue the conversation.

4. Coping with Stress

Experiencing stress can cause emotions and feelings of all shapes and sizes. It can even cause serious health conditions if not properly managed.

Today's teens and young adults face various stressors never seen before; most notable among them are social media and the 24-hour news cycle.

The pressure teens always feel to present themselves perfectly online and process the bombardment of information continuously coming their way can take a mental toll.

So before we go any further, say to yourself, "It's OK not to be perfect." It's 100% true, and honestly, no one is. No matter how successful or well put together they seem, every person experiences insecurities.

Some ways to handle stress are the same as managing strong emotions, such as taking a walk, listening to music, talking to a trusted person, and engaging in deep breathing or yoga.

One of the best ways to deal with stress is to unplug for a while. Turn your phone, computer, and TV off. Read a book, do a puzzle, draw, make art, play a game with a friend or a sibling, or enjoy a cup of coffee or a meal with someone close.

When we can reconnect with our lives and engage in something soothing and enjoyable, it automatically releases endorphins, making us feel better.

Some other things you can do to relieve stress include knowing when to take a break, avoiding excess caffeine, and eating healthy. If you have been working on your big paper for two hours straight, it might be time to get up from your desk and stretch or walk instead of pouring yourself another cup of coffee.

Engaging in regular physical activity and making sure you get enough sleep are also crucial. You may think staying up an extra two hours to cram for a test is your best bet, but getting adequate sleep is going to make you feel much better than attempting to take that test on four hours of sleep.

We can't always avoid people we don't get along with, but we can do our part and not seek those individuals out. If someone close to you seems to enjoy pushing your buttons, recognize those triggers and do not respond. If the person realizes they won't get a reaction out of you, eventually, they will stop trying.

If a specific class at school keeps you up at night, talk to the teacher or professor. See if there is tutoring available or, if possible, if you can drop the class. If dropping the course is not an option, showing the teacher you are concerned and engaged will help them better understand where you are coming from and be better equipped to help you.

When possible, take steps to eliminate the things causing you stress. While this is not always possible, it is worth looking at if something is causing you undue amounts of stress.

5. Missing Your Friends & Family

Most teens either end up going to college or eventually moving out of their home, possibly even far away from the people they grew up with and knew their whole lives. Dealing with feelings of loneliness and missing loved ones can be tough.

One thing that can help is for you to focus on your new adventure. If you decided to go to college in California, 2,000 miles away from home, reflect on why you chose this school and this location.

Making a list of all the reasons you wanted to make this change in the first place can help affirm your decision.

If you are in a new place, go out and explore. Walk around the neighborhood or the city or get in your car and go for a drive. Find some new spots to hang out, like a local coffee shop or bookstore, join a gym or health club, or sign up for a class.

Remember that your friends and family are missing you too, but they also want you to be happy! They will be excited to hear about your new adventure!

Luckily for modern teens, technology makes contacting those you miss lightning fast. With a press of a button, you can FaceTime, Zoom, send a text, email, or make a phone call. Social media allows us to stay connected to those we miss, even if they are on the other side of the world.

It can also help to schedule a regular virtual date with someone that you are missing. If you know that you will talk to your person every Wednesday and Saturday at 5 p.m., it gives you something to look forward to and reassurance that you will see and speak with them again soon.

Writing them an old-fashioned letter can also help, even if you don't send it to them. The act of writing how you are feeling down can be therapeutic and beneficial.

Consider mailing notes and letters to each other. These days, we rarely get any mail worth reading, so knowing you can expect a letter can be fun and exciting.

PROBLEM-SOLVING & DECISION MAKING

1. Facing Problems

Nobody likes having problems or dealing with them, but they are an unfortunate part of life. The best thing you can do is learn how to face a problem head-on instead of running away or hiding from it.

It may be scary, but facing a problem and dealing with it will likely make you feel much better in the end.

The first step in facing a problem is naming it. Once you name it, you can deal with it. The next step is to list what scares you about the situation. What is the worst that can happen if you face this problem?

Let's say you borrowed your mom's car and accidentally scraped the side of it, and it has a small dent in it now. Facing mom can be pretty scary. So, knowing your mom, what is the worst that could happen? Is it that you get grounded for a week? Maybe it will be that you lose car privileges for a time. Or perhaps she'll be upset and yell, AND you'll be grounded.

None of those options are pleasant, but writing down your worst fears can help.

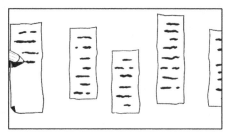

Next, write down what will happen if you DON'T deal with it. In the situation above, will your mom receive the news better if you are honest and upfront versus if she finds out about it and has to confront you? If you lie, will the punishment be worse?

After you have written these two lists, decide what you are going to do. Maybe you tell mom and then offer to pay for the dent to be repaired. Perhaps you tell mom that you know you made a mistake: take responsibility and accept whatever consequence she decides. Whatever you decide, have a plan.

Finally, pat yourself on the back for following through. Okay, so maybe you don't get to drive the car for a week, but you were honest, which should make you feel good and make you more careful driving next time.

2. Discovering the Problem

Facing a problem is great if you know what it is, but what if you are not exactly sure what it is? Before you can begin solving a problem, you need to understand what exactly is wrong.

Some problems may be medical and require tests and doctor visits to figure out. Any time you are experiencing symptoms that are not normal for you, write them down. If your symptoms reoccur consistently, you may need to schedule a doctor's appointment.

Some problems may be school-related. If you are struggling in a class but can't figure out why, schedule a meeting with your teacher or professor. They may shed some light on why they think you are struggling and help you work towards a solution.

To discover the problem, you may need to analyze the situation. Sometimes you can do that on your own, and sometimes you will need outside input.

For example, maybe it is difficult to focus on your homework or practicing the piano. When you stop and analyze the situation, you realize you're hungry and the kids playing outside are making a lot of noise, making it difficult to concentrate.

Now you've identified the problem and what is causing it! Time for a solution!

3. Coming Up with Solutions

Discovering the problem is step one; finding the solution is step two.

Finding the solution to a problem may feel much like solving a mystery or puzzle, but there are steps you can take to help you work your way towards the best possible solution.

The first of these steps is writing down every possible solution - even write down the ones that may seem ludicrous; you never know, they may spark a more realistic idea.

Next, analyze these solutions. If you need help with either of these steps, consider asking your parents or friends for advice.

Narrow down the solutions to the one that seems the most likely to work and the most realistic. It's great to say, "Well, if I won $25,000 in the lottery, I could buy a new car to replace mine that keeps breaking down," and it's true, you could, but it is not very realistic.

Once you have decided on a solution, plan the steps needed to put that solution in motion.

If you are still facing the same struggles after a predetermined amount of time, head back to the drawing board and analyze the situation again. Some problems will require trial and error to solve.

4. Making a Decision on Your Own

As you reach adulthood, you will be required to make more and more decisions on your own. Of course, you can always seek out advice from your parents. But ultimately, final decisions will have to be made by you.

Some of these decisions will be minor, and others much more life-altering. Once you are eighteen, your mom and dad cannot stop you from getting a tattoo, but does that mean you really should?

So how do you make a decision?

First, make a list of all the pros and cons of any big decisions you need to make. For example, if you are trying to decide between two colleges, your list may look like this:

PROS

University of Miami	NYU
Warm weather	Lots of history
Close to the beach	New York City
Nightlife	Nightlife
35% acceptance rate	16% acceptance rate

CONS

University of Miami	NYU
Hot	Cold Winters
Far away from home	Expensive
Party school	Lots of distractions
Large class size	Lack of financial aid

After listing out all of the pros and cons, consider your values and goals as you weigh your options. This will help you decide which of these are the most important or non-negotiable.

Once you have weighed out all the possibilities, find someone to talk it through with you. Having someone to bounce your ideas around with can help, especially as you hear ideas and thoughts filtered through someone else.

5. Decisions & Consequences

When making a decision, one thing to keep in mind is that ALL decisions have consequences. Most decisions are small and inconsequential, but some decisions can have MAJOR consequences.

Unfortunately, we don't always know when a decision will make a big difference or not. It could be that your decision to stop and get coffee one day makes you five minutes later for work than you would typically be. That same decision could also prevent you from being in a car crash, or in five years, have you married to the barista who served you the coffee. The thing is, often, we will never know.

Since you can't live your life agonizing over every little decision, there is no benefit to weighing the pros and cons of everything you do. When you need to make a more significant decision, weighing out possible consequences, both negative and positive, has value.

Consequences are not always a bad thing. If you are nervous about taking a big risk - could the positive consequences prove monumental? Do you take the leap and apply to Yale and then get in? Do you take the bus to New York for the audition and land a part in a Broadway production? Do you say no to getting in a car with your friend who has been drinking and then live after they crash their car?

In the end, you will be the one who makes decisions for yourself. Taking the time to consider the consequences before you leap is always a smart idea.

SECTION EIGHT:

BEHAVIORAL SKILLS

1. Morals and Convictions

If you went to Sunday school, Hebrew school, read Aesop's Fables and fairy tales as a child or participated in any religious practices growing up, you have likely heard the word moral.

When you are a person with morals, you understand right from wrong and choose to make the right decisions because you know what is fair and just.

Every human being does things from time to time that goes against their morals. People lie; they don't stand up for someone being teased; they might have stolen a candy bar from the convenience store; ignored a text because someone was getting on their nerves; or slacked off at work and did the minimum amount possible.

A conviction is what guides a moral. For example, if you believe that people should always tell the truth, no matter what, you probably do not lie. If you think that hard work is the way to achieve results, you will follow through with your responsibilities no matter how much you don't want to do them.

Morals and convictions are your compasses to help you stay on the right path. It is important to stay true to your beliefs, but you also need to make sure your convictions don't hurt anyone else.

Suppose you believe that only certain people should be allowed to marry or that only certain genders can do a job or perform a role. In that case, you are entitled to that belief, but you should not use convictions as a means to disparage and harm other people.

2. Staying True to Yourself

Peer pressure. You've heard of it, and it is very real. While it may be extreme in the adolescent and teen years, it never really goes away. Learning how to stay strong when it matters is vital to developing coping skills when under peer pressure.

One way to avoid peer pressure is by possessing a deep understanding of your morals and convictions.

As a line from the Broadway hit Hamilton goes:

If you stand for nothing, Burr, what will you fall for?

One way to discover where you stand on many issues is to ask yourself some questions about moral or ethical situations. Here are some examples:

- If someone is starving, is it okay to steal food? Why or why not?
- Is it ever okay to lie? If so, what are the circumstances?
- If a large group of people decide something is right, can they be wrong?

- If one religion says something is okay, but another says it is not, which one is correct? Can they both be right or both be wrong?
- Is it ever okay to physically harm someone? If so, in what situation?
- Does it matter if someone underage drinks or smokes? Do you believe legal ages are set for a good reason? Why or why not?
- Can war be justified? Why or why not?

When faced with a tough decision, there are a series of questions you can ask yourself:

- Is it safe?
- Is it legal?
- Would I do this in front of my mom or dad?
- How will this make me feel about myself?
- Is it fair and balanced?
- How will this affect others?
- Do I want to do this?
- If no one were watching or encouraging me, would I still do this?
- Am I willing to accept the consequences of these actions?

Saying no to our peers can be difficult at any age, but it can be particularly challenging for teens. If you understand your beliefs and why you hold them, making the right decision will be more comfortable, even if it is not easy.

If, after all of this, the only question left is, "Will they still want to be my friends if I disagree?" and the answer is "no," then these people are likely not real friends in the first place.

3. Mistakes

When you make a mistake, the first step is admitting that you made one. After you recognize the mistake, discover what you need to do to rectify it. In some cases, you will not do anything. For example, let's say you were making a cake and you used baking soda instead of baking powder. Now the cake tastes terrible, so you admit your mistake, everyone has a laugh, and no harm is done.

Sometimes, however, mistakes can cause harm to others or negatively affect other people. In that case, it is essential to own the mistake and attempt to fix it.

Suppose you promised your mom you'd babysit your sister, but then forgot and went out with your friends. Now you get an angry telephone call fifteen minutes after you were supposed to be home. Your reaction is to get home as soon as possible, apologize to your mom, and figure out how you will avoid making that mistake again. In the future, you could set a reminder on your cell phone or use a datebook.

After making a mistake, you need to make amends. Experts say that young children should never be forced to apologize because the words mean nothing to them. Instead, we need to encourage children to fix their mistakes. Consider this scenario: Billy knocked over Susie's tower, and then he helped her build it again. See how it works?

And lastly, some of your mistakes will only affect you. You didn't put enough time in on your biology paper and received a C. Accept that it was your fault and no one else's. Then make a promise to yourself that next time you have a big project due, you will carve out more time and start sooner.

4. Apologies

If mistakes warrant it, be prepared to say you are sorry. Accepting a mistake and then apologizing is a defining feature of a mature and responsible individual.

There are many ways to apologize. The situation and person you are apologizing to will stipulate some of the factors in your apology.

The way you apologize to your girlfriend because you left her waiting 30 minutes with no text or phone call is going to be different than how you apologize to your boss if you showed up late to work again.

When you begin an apology, it should start with what you are sorry for:

I am sorry I am late and didn't text or call you.

91

Next, state why your action was wrong:

Since I didn't call, I made you worried and upset.

Third, take responsibility:

I am responsible for this, and it is my fault.

Fourth ask how you can make it better or suggest a way to make it better:

What can I do that would make you feel better?

Fifth, let them know how you will change it in the future.

I promise if I am running late again by more than a few minutes, I will call you.

Finally, ask for forgiveness and thank them for listening to you.

HOW TO APOLOGIZE

(1)	Say what you are sorry for.	"I am sorry for..."
(2)	Say why it was wrong.	"It was wrong because..."
(3)	Accept full responsibility.	I accept full responsibility for what I did/said.
(4)	Ask how to make amends.	"How can I make this better?"
(5)	Commit to not doing this again.	"Moving forward, I promise to..."
(6)	Ask for forgiveness.	"Will you accept my apology?"
(7)	Thank them.	"Thank you for bringing this to my attention."

☹ THESE ARE NOT APOLOGIES:

- I'm sorry you feel that way.
- I'm sorry you misinterpreted what I said.
- You misinterpreted what I meant.

- I'm sorry but...
- What about that time you...
- It was your fault that I...

Avoid making apologies that sound like accusations such as *I'm sorry you didn't understand; I am sorry I made you feel that way; I am sorry this happened; I only did that because you did,* etc.

The goal of an apology is to make the person feel better about the mistake you made, not for you to justify all the reasons you made a mistake in the first place.

5. Minding Your Ps & Qs

Good manners are essential, not just because it is a polite way to act but because it is a way to show respect and kindness to those around you. The origin of the phrase "Mind your Ps and Qs" is not definitive, but in general, it means to be on your best behavior.

You should say please anytime you ask someone for something, even if it is just for a pack of ketchup from the fast-food clerk. On the flip side, you need to say thank you every time someone does something for you. Yes, even when your sister brings your laundry upstairs for you.

One important thing to keep in mind is that different cultures have different customs that they consider good manners. In the United States, shaking someone's hand and making eye contact is considered good manners. However, in other cultures, children are taught it is rude to maintain direct eye contact, and instead, they are taught to look at each other's necks.

In general, if you follow the manners and customs you are familiar with, you will be just fine. Still, if you are in a situation where you interact with people from a different culture, you can show them respect by learning about their culture and customs ahead of time.

6. Asking for Help

For some, asking for help is a challenge. Sometimes we don't want to admit that we don't have all the answers. Maybe we're embarrassed to raise our hand in class to ask a question. Perhaps the question is private and personal, and we don't know who to ask.

There are some guidelines to take to heart when asking for help to make you feel more confident.

- First, don't apologize for asking for help. When you apologize, you are cementing in your brain that there is something wrong with asking for help - there isn't!

- Second, be clear about what you are asking for help with. If you are vague, the other person might not understand and may provide poor advice.

  o It may help to write down your thoughts to know what you want to say if you are nervous.

- When possible, ask for help in person. It helps the person we are talking with to see our faces and hear the emotion in our voices.

  o If needed, you can email or call to schedule a time to talk to them in person.
  o You can also use FaceTime or Zoom if an in-person meeting is not an option.

- Depending on the situation, be prepared to show that you have already tried to solve the problem on your own. This is especially helpful with teachers and bosses.
- Finally, follow up. If the person you asked for help says they'll get back to you in a few days, there is nothing wrong with checking back in.

  o They could have forgotten, never sent the email, or were busy and didn't realize how much time had passed.

SECTION NINE:

SOCIAL SKILLS

1. Engaging in a Hobby

Once we leave high school and enter adulthood, building meaningful friendships can be much harder. One way to make new social connections and friends is to engage in a hobby.

There are clubs, organizations, and teams for just about any hobby. Many of them can be found through social media channels. Most community colleges also offer non-credit classes that focus on different skills and interests.

If you are looking for a way to build some social interaction while also engaging in a new or familiar hobby, check out your local YMCA or parks department. They often offer everything from dance classes to group painting to intramural sports.

If you are more of a homebody, consider joining an online group. These groups are a great way to find support and tips for your hobby, and they can also be a way for you to share your expertise on a subject.

Libraries are another trusted source when looking for hobbies to engage in. Activities hosted by the library are often free or cost a minimal fee. Sign-up for your local library's newsletter, and you may find your next yoga class or book club.

2. Making and Maintaining Friendships

When developing or maintaining a friendship, one key component is honesty. While we often worry that people won't like us as ourselves, the people we genuinely want to be around will accept our faults and quirks.

Often, we bond with people over shared interests; you may attend the same church or be on the same soccer team. If you find yourself drawn to a person, make a point of talking to them when you see them.

Perhaps you could offer them a compliment: "Your solo sounded great in chorus today." Or mention something you notice: "Hey, those shoes are cool; where did you get them?" Making someone feel good about themselves is a great ice breaker.

If you're looking to hang out, you can always ask the person if they want to grab a meal after a gathering or maybe head over to the local music shop to flip through some old records. Whatever your shared interest is, use that to build the relationship.

Remember that creating a true friendship takes time and that the person you are working towards being friends with might be just as nervous as you are. Everyone has insecurities, so what seems like reluctance from someone may be nerves.

The most important thing is to be yourself. You don't need to divulge all your deepest secrets on day one, but don't shy away from what makes you, you.

3. Healthy Family Relationships

As you enter and go through your teen years, your relationship with your parents and siblings is likely to change.

Teenagers think they know everything. It's harsh to hear it, but you do, and the truth is you barely know a fraction of what there is to know. Your parents don't know everything either, but they have been where you are (maybe not exactly, but close), and they have a lot more life experience to back up their knowledge.

While you should not blindly accept everything an adult says to you, mutual respect needs to develop between teens and their parents.

When you show your parents respect, in most cases, they will offer it to you in return. The same goes for yelling, door slamming, and frustration. Keeping a level head while talking or listening is essential. If you have strong feelings about something that you don't see eye-to-eye on with your parents, ask them if you can sit down and talk with them calmly about the topic.

Perhaps you want to try out for the school play, but your parents are afraid it will interfere with your schoolwork. Or maybe you want to get a part-time job instead of playing softball this year. In the end, it is important to remember your parents have the final say. As disagreeable as it may be, learning to accept your parents' final decisions will also set you up for accepting protocols from bosses and other authority figures.

If you have younger siblings, your relationship is likely going to change with them as well. As a teen, your social calendar and schoolwork will both expand, leaving less time to hang out with younger siblings.

When possible, make time for them and include them in something you're doing, especially if they are only a few years younger. While you may not think it is fun to have your "kid sister" following you around, your siblings are the people who will be by your side longer than any others in your life.

Consider finding a way for the two of you to do something special together, like watching a movie or hanging out at the mall once in a while to let them know they are still important to you.

Maintaining a healthy and positive relationship with your siblings when you are a teen will benefit you as an adult, even if you can't see it now.

5. Respecting Different Opinions

One thing that is guaranteed is that you will meet many people in your life who hold and express different opinions than yours. When you are young and first meet people outside the world you grew up in, these differences can sometimes feel shocking or upsetting.

When meeting someone who holds a different opinion than yours, it is important not to judge them right away, even if that opinion is somewhat offensive. Not all people we meet will have had access to the same experiences, information, knowledge, and relationships that we have had. Since these are all factors that can affect someone's opinions, understanding where someone is coming from is key to accepting them and their opinions.

You do not need to agree with, adopt, or like the opinions of others you meet, but it is important to show respect. You and your morals will decide what opinions you find entirely unacceptable. Regardless of beliefs, it should be possible to maintain a relationship with most people you meet that have different views.

One way to better understand someone's opinions is to ask them about it. Having a frank conversation with the person and asking them to explain why they hold their beliefs can be an eye-opening experience.

It is dangerous to surround ourselves with people who only think just like we do. Getting to know people from different walks of life, backgrounds, and different experiences provides us with a richer view of the world. Exposure to these views enables us to have an open mind and empathy for others.

If someone close to you holds an opinion you find offensive, ask them if you may explain why you feel the way you do. Talking is often the best way to resolve issues and understand another's point of view.

6. Party Etiquette

Now that you're all grown up (or almost), you may be invited to parties, or you may even find yourself hosting one. No, we're not talking about the kind of frat parties you hear about in college. We mean a social event where you ask friends and perhaps family to come together to mingle or celebrate.

Step one is deciding what type of party you are having. Is it a birthday party, or did you move into a new apartment? Maybe it's your mom's 50th birthday, and you want to surprise her with a get-together. Whatever your reason, that will be your starting point.

Once you know the reason for your party, decide if you are going to have a theme. Is it an Oscar Night party, or are you having a fun beach luau? Announcing your theme on the invite will help your guests know what to expect. If there is no theme and it's merely a get-together - then that's okay too.

The next item to put together is your guest list. If the party is for your mom's birthday, the guest list will likely include her friends and family members. If the party is for your 18th birthday, the list will look different.

When creating a guest list, it is essential to think about how different people will interact with each other. You also need to make sure you are not hurting anyone's feelings. This may mean inviting people you are not 100% fond of, especially if the party is for someone else or to mark an important event such as your graduation. Your uncle Jim may get on your nerves, but it would be rude to exclude him.

Your guests will expect there to be some kind of food and drink at the party. If you are not serving a meal, you should write, "light refreshments will be served." Hosting a party can be costly, so one way to save money is to invite each guest to bring a different dish. You can assign a category to each guest, such as dessert, appetizer, salad, or you can leave it open and hope for the best (but you may end up with 15 different types of dip and chips).

When you are the party host, you must mingle and talk to everyone, and you should thank them for coming. Hiding in the corner is a no-no.

Hosting a party is a lot of work. Even for a small gathering of a few friends, you will need to put time and effort into the preparations. In the end, the work is worth it, though! Parties are a great way of creating life-long fond memories with friends and family.

SECTION TEN:

CLOTHING

1. Doing the Laundry

Now that you are learning how to become more responsible, it is time you learned how to do your laundry. Hopefully, if your mom or dad hasn't taught you yet, this information will set you on the right path.

One of the most important things you need to do when preparing your laundry is to read clothing labels.

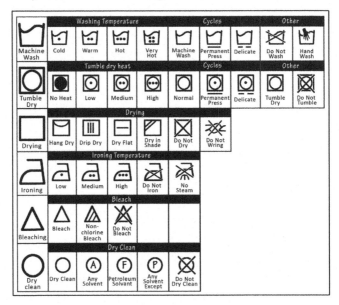

Labels speak their own language. Learning how to decipher the different pictures will make your clothing last longer and prevent you from ruining your items.

It is important to pay attention to the items that say do not tumble dry, dry clean only, or wash in cold, as altering these directions could lead to damage and potentially ruin the article of clothing.

If you do not have an outdoor space to hang-dry your clothes, you can purchase devices and drying racks suitable for smaller spaces.

Each washing and drying machine is different, so there is no one-size-fits-all option when teaching you how to use the machines. The knobs and buttons are usually clearly labeled, so be sure to read the settings before you begin.

You should check for the water temperature, the water level, and the wash setting.

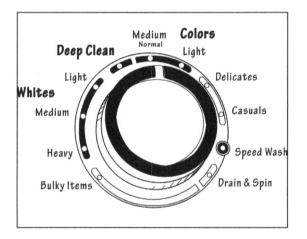

Some clothing labels will tell you which cycle to wash items on. Pay particular attention if the article of clothing says to wash on delicate.

Most clothing is safe to wash in cold water, but dark or brightly colored clothing should always be washed in cold, as hot water can make the colors run or fade. It is recommended that you wash your lights and darks separately.

Items that are 100% cotton should be dried on a low setting or allowed to air dry to prevent them from shrinking.

Some clothing will need to be hand-washed. To wash items by hand, fill a basin or the sink with room temperature water. Add the laundry detergent as the water is filling, much like a bubble bath. Next, add the clothing you wish to wash. You can agitate the water with your hand for several minutes to mix the water, detergent, and clothing. Rinse the items well with room temperature water until all the soap is rinsed out. Lastly, wring the items out to remove all the excess water and hang them to dry.

HOW TO WASH CLOTHES BY HAND

1 — SEPARATE LIGHT AND DARK CLOTHES

2 — FULL TWO TUBS WITH WATER

3 — ADD DETERGENT IN ONE TUB

4 — WASH CLOTHES

5 — RINSE IN CLEAR WATER

6 — WRING OUT CLOTHES

7 — LET CLOTHES DRY

2. Ironing Clothing

Depending on the material, some clothing may require ironing. Fabrics such as cotton and linen are more prone to wrinkling than nylon or acrylic.

Many irons will have the heat setting directly on them. It is important to adjust the setting appropriately so the fabric does not burn. Some materials will require steam to smooth out the fabric completely. Irons have a small compartment you fill with water, creating steam when a small button is depressed.

Cotton fabrics, especially, need to be damp, so consider taking cotton fabrics out of the dryer to iron before they are dry.

Ironing fabrics inside out can help save them from fading or scorch marks. When ironing delicate fabrics, place a cloth on top as a barrier of protection between the material and the iron.

IRONING INSTRUCTIONS ACCORDING TO FABRIC		TEMP	STEAM
NATURAL FIBERS	Cotton (denim, muslin, calico, chintz): Iron on high heat while still damp. If the fabric is dry, pre-moisten it with a spray bottle or use the spray button on your iron to dampen the fabric. Use steam and spray if necessary.	🔥	💨
	Linen: Iron while still damp on the wrong side using high heat. If the fabric is dry, pre-moisten it with a spray bottle or use the spray button on your iron to dampen the fabric.	🔥	💨
	Wool (cashmere, flannel): Use a pressing cloth and iron on the wrong side of the fabric on medium heat.	🔥	💨
	Silk: Use a medium heat setting and dry-iron the silk on the wrong side of the fabric. To press a silk tie, lay it on top of a pressing cloth, right-side facing down, then press.	🔥	💨
SYNTHETIC FIBERS	Polyester: Iron while still damp. Pre-moisten it with a spray bottle or use the spray button on your iron to dampen the fabric. Use low or medium heat.	🔥	💨
	Nylon: Use low heat and dry iron without steam. Use spray if necessary.	🔥	💨
	Acetate: Using low heat, dry iron without steam on the wrong side of the fabric.	🔥	💨
	Acrylic: With the iron on low heat, dry iron without steam on the wrong side of the fabric. Use spray if necessary.	🔥	💨

3. Folding Clothes

Now that you have washed and dried your clothes, ironed, and hung what you can into your closet, you need to know how to fold the remaining items. There are varying opinions on how to fold almost every item of clothing, so it's not a matter of right or wrong but a matter of preference.

- **Socks:** Method one involves laying both socks on top of each other and merely folding them in half. With method two, lay the socks on top of each other and roll the cuffs down. The third method involves laying one sock on top of the other and rolling them into a small log shape.

- **T-shirts**: If you like your shirts to be compact and folded as if they were on the shelves of a clothing boutique, here is a simple method to achieve that goal.

  - Start by laying your t-shirt face-up on a flat surface. Next, fold over one sleeve towards the collar. Next, fold over the same side in a straight line, centering it with the collar. Do the same on the opposite side. Finally, fold the shirt in half to make a rectangle.

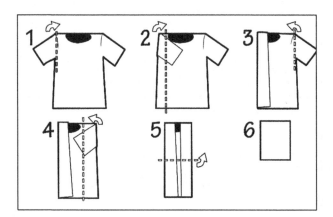

- **Bras**: This is a trick question because you shouldn't fold bras. Only cotton or lycra sports bras should be folded in half and placed in your drawer. Bras with a cup shape should be placed front to back, stacked gently on top of one another to keep their shape.

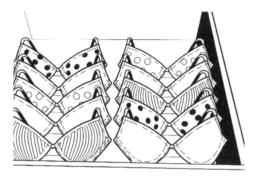

- **Pants:** With most slacks and dress pants, you're going to want to hang them in your closet to prevent them from wrinkling, but you may choose to fold your sweatpants, jeans, or pajama pants, so here is a quick and easy method to save space.

  o Lay them on a flat surface and fold one leg on top of the other. From the bottom, fold the leg about a third of the way up. From there, fold them over again and for the final fold, do a slight roll. *Voila!* Space-saving folded pants.

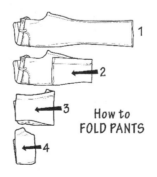

How to
FOLD PANTS

4. How to Tie a Tie

There are various styles of tie knots you can learn if you'll be wearing a tie regularly or on special occasions. While the workplace is becoming less formal than decades past, there are still plenty of occasions and offices where wearing a tie is expected.

Below is a diagram of a standard method of tying a tie. Let's walk through it step by step.

- Hang the tie around your neck with the backside facing up and so that the fatter end is slightly longer than the thin end.
- Pull the fat side under the thin side like an "X" and then wrap it around the place where the two pieces cross. The front side of the tie should face out as you wrap it around.
- You will have a little loop at the base of your neck. Pull the piece you just wrapped around back up and tuck the fat side of the tie, face-out through the loop, and gently pull down.
- Tighten the tie so that it feels firm but not uncomfortable around your neck.

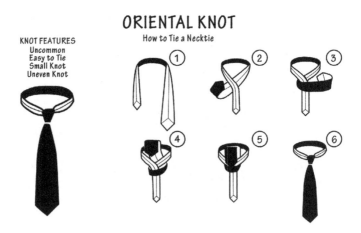

ORIENTAL KNOT

KNOT FEATURES
Uncommon
Easy to Tie
Small Knot
Uneven Knot

How to Tie a Necktie

Don't feel discouraged if it takes several attempts to get the tie adjusted correctly. If it helps, practice in front of a mirror.

5. Cleaning Your Shoes

Yes! Shoes can be cleaned, and we don't mean throwing them in the washer and dryer. How you clean your shoes will depend on the material they are made of, such as leather, rubber, canvas, etc.

Before you clean any pair of shoes, it is recommended you remove the laces. It makes things easier not to have them in the way. For some shoes, the cleaning solutions might damage the laces.

- **Leather:** Use a soft cloth or brush to remove any excess dirt. Use warm water and dish soap to clean the shoe's surface. Use another clean, damp cloth to remove any dirt residue. Dry them with a soft towel, and then apply a leather conditioner. The conditioner helps protect your shoes from scuffs and other marks. Allow your leather shoes to air dry but not in the sun or near a heater, as the heat can crack the leather.
- **Canvas Shoes:** Canvas shoes with no leather trim and a rubber sole can be washed in your washing machine by placing them in a mesh bag and washing them on the gentle cycle with jeans or towels. Attempt to remove stains and excess mud ahead of time as mud can clog your washing machine. If you need to wash them by hand, use a solution of warm water and a dash of laundry detergent. Use a soft bristle brush or sponge to scrub away dirt and stains. Rinse them with clean water and use a clean cloth or sponge to dab excess water. Whether you use the washing machine or hand wash, allow canvas shoes to air dry.

- **Rubber Shoes:** First, remove any excess dirt. Next, use a dry brush to remove any loose dirt. To clean the rubber, mix warm water and dish soap and use a brush or sponge to scrub. Use a clean, damp sponge or cloth to remove any soap residue and dry them with a clean cloth.

6. Sewing a Button

Knowing how to mend a button on a shirt or pair of pants can save you a lot of time and money, and it's easy to do.

If a button has fallen off a piece of clothing, put it somewhere safe, so you have it when needed. If you have lost it, check the garment's inside to see if additional buttons are sewn there. Some clothing will come with an extra button or two; keep these, especially if the button is particularly unique.

If the button you are replacing is not visible, then it does not matter if it matches as long as it is the right size. Too small a button will slip right through the buttonhole, and too large won't fit. Most buttons have either two or four holes. The sewing technique is the same for both button styles.

Choose a thread similar in color to either the button or clothing garment. Thread your needle by poking the thread through the eye of the needle. You want to pull roughly 2-3 inches of extra thread through.

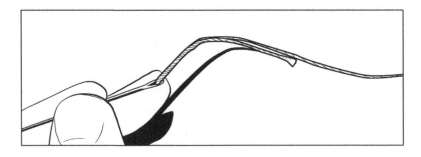

Tie a knot in your thread at the far end, leaving yourself about 10-12 inches to work with. Place the button on the clothing and, starting on the underside, push the needle and thread through the first hole, pulling gently until the knot is flush against the clothing's back.

Take the needle down through the next hole and pull the thread all the way through. Repeat this up and down pattern several times until the button feels securely attached.

To finish attaching the button, push the needle and thread through the stitches' backside two or three times, making a final knot. Tie the thread and then cut off any excess.

A simple sewing kit containing needles, different shades of thread, small scissors, and extra buttons can be purchased for around $15 and is a great item to keep around your home.

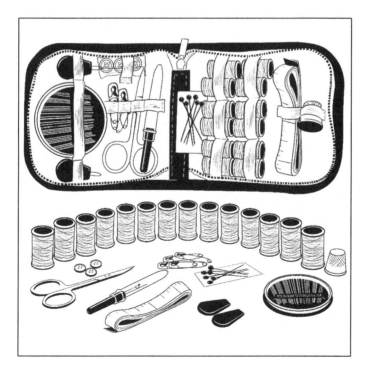

SECTION ELEVEN:

HOME MAINTENANCE

1. Circuit Breakers

A circuit breaker is a safety device in your home that prevents damage to electrical items when there is a surge of electricity. When a breaker detects a surge, it will automatically shut off and cut power to the device.

A surge can happen when too many devices are plugged into the same outlet, during lightning storms or power outages, and due to damaged or exposed wiring.

Suppose the surge happened because you had too many devices in use at once. In that case, you should reconsider using those devices at the same time and invest in surge protector cords/ outlets.

If it seems to happen frequently, you may need an electrician to check the wiring in your home.

To reset your circuit breaker, you will need to locate the circuit box. These are usually found in the basement, garage, or utility-type room.

The tripped circuit will be flipped in the opposite direction than the others. Push it in the same direction as the other breakers to reset it.

If your circuit box is not labeled, it is beneficial to do so. To test each breaker one at a time, turn all the lights on, have items plugged into the outlet, and turn off each breaker one at a time. Once you identify what that circuit is attached to (i.e., kitchen, washing machine, bathroom), use a pencil or pen to write it on tape or the pre-affixed label. If possible, have a friend or family member help so you are not running from room to room each time you flip a breaker.

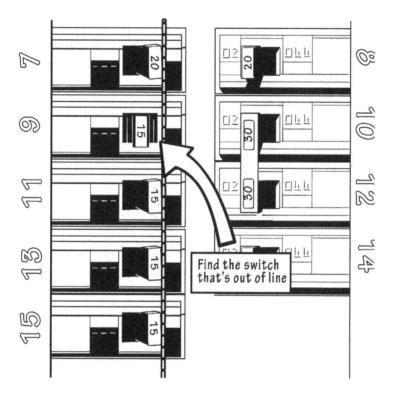

Find the switch that's out of line

2. Water Line, Water Heater, & Furnace

❏ Water Line

If a pipe bursts or you are heading out of town, you will need to know how to turn off the main water line to your home. The main water line will likely have two valves, one outside and one inside. Turn a faucet on in the house, so you know water is flowing.

There are two types of valves: a ball valve and a gate valve. To turn off a gate valve, turn the dial clockwise. To turn off a ball valve, the lever should be facing down. It is recommended that if you cannot do it by hand, contact a plumber. Forcing it could damage the pipes or the valve.

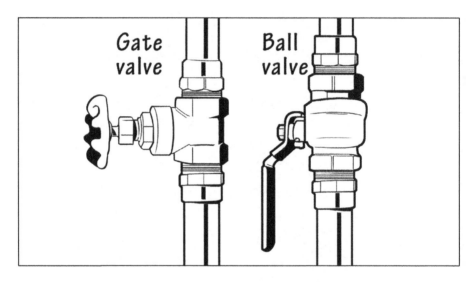

❑ Water Heater

You guessed it! The water heater heats the water in your home. If your water heater goes bottoms up, you will be taking cold showers until it is fixed.

There are electric water heaters and gas water heaters. Much like a stove, a gas water heater relies on a pilot light to heat the gas, which in turn warms your water. While it is possible to relight the pilot light yourself, you must follow the manufacturer's instructions to avoid injury. If you do not feel comfortable, contact a professional to do it for you.

If you have an electric water heater and the temperatures are dropping, check your power supply first to make sure it didn't accidentally become unplugged or that your breaker hasn't tripped.

If your water is consistently lukewarm or spikes between hot and cold in a matter of moments, it is probably time to have a plumber take a look.

❑ Furnace

The furnace is what keeps your home warm and is connected to your central heating system. Furnace problems often strike when the weather is cold, so look out for the following:

- frozen pipes caused by dropping temperatures
- dirty filters
- broken thermostat
- faulty pilot light
- carbon monoxide leaks

If your furnace is malfunctioning, especially if you suspect a carbon monoxide leak, turn it off immediately and schedule to have a professional take a look. There should be a switch in the same room that looks like a light switch; simply switch that off. If there is no switch, turn it off by flipping the breaker.

If you have a gas furnace, you can turn off the gas by locating the gas line and turning off the valve.

It is recommended to have a carbon monoxide detector near your furnace. Carbon monoxide is odorless but deadly, so it is crucial to have a working carbon monoxide detector.

3. Using a Fire Extinguisher

Although you will likely never need to use one, knowing how to use a fire extinguisher could save your life.

If you don't have a fire extinguisher and an oil fire breaks out in the kitchen while cooking, **DO NOT put water onto an oil fire.** The best way to stop an oil fire without a fire extinguisher is to smother it.

- Turn off the heat source
- Smother with a lid or cookie sheet
- Throw salt or baking soda onto it

You need a Class B fire extinguisher to put out an oil fire. Small aerosol fire extinguishers can be purchased and stored in your kitchen.

To use a standard fire extinguisher, remember **PASS:**

- Pull the Pin
- Aim the nozzle
- Squeeze the lever slowly
- Sweep side to side

4. Fixing a Running Toilet

If your toilet is running, your water bill can quickly escalate. A running toilet is identified by the sound of water filling the tank (like right after you've flushed) continuously. This sound means water is running from the mainline, through your toilet tank, and back out again.

One inexpensive way to check to see if your toilet is running is by waiting a few moments after it has been flushed and then looking inside the tank. If water is still filling the tank several minutes later, you have a leak.

The first thing to do is check the flapper: the circular rubber piece at the bottom of the tank. Using something long, like a ruler or dowel rod, press down on the flapper; if the noise stops, you have found your leak.

THE DIFFERENT PARTS OF THE TOILET

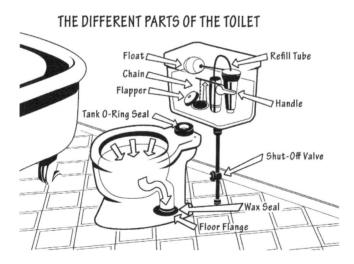

Float
Chain
Flapper
Tank O-Ring Seal
Refill Tube
Handle
Shut-Off Valve
Wax Seal
Floor Flange

If the flapper is the issue, you should be able to replace it yourself. Before you begin, you need to look at the flapper and purchase the same type and size. It might be beneficial to bring the old one with you to the hardware store for identification.

119

Start by turning off the water to the toilet by twisting the shut-off valve clockwise to the off position. Hold the handle down and allow all the water to drain out of the tank.

Next, unhook the chain that attaches the flapper to the handle lever and remove the flapper. You will have to look closely at the bottom of the tank to see how it is attached - most have pegs or ears attached to the side. If a ring attachment goes around the overflow tube, you will need to cut it off.

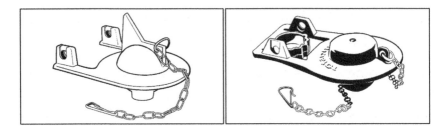

Affix the new flapper and attach the chain to the flush handle. The chain should have a little bit of slack, but not so much that it rests at the bottom of the tank. Turn the water back on and allow the tank to fill. Test the new flapper by flushing the toilet a few times.

If you still have a leak after replacing the flapper, you may need a plumber to come in and take a look.

5. Quick Household Fixes

Learning how to take care of some household repairs will come in handy as you get ready to venture out on your own, so let's cover a few of the basics.

- **Screwdrivers:** There are several types of screwdrivers, but the main two you will probably need are a Phillip's Head and Flat Head. Owning a small screwdriver set is an excellent investment for tightening loose screws around the home.

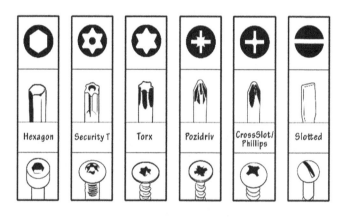

- **Light Bulbs:** Yup, light bulbs come in all different shapes, sizes, colors, and brightness. If you need to replace a light bulb, turn off the power source and unscrew the dead bulb. At the base of the bulb, it should tell you what wattage and size it is. When in doubt, take the bulb to the store with you.
- **Hanging Objects:** If you plan to decorate, you may wish to hang up pictures, mirrors, shelves, or other artwork in your home. To avoid damaging the walls, here are a few tips.

121

o For small and light items, consider using hanging strips. There are hanging strips designed to hold everything from 0.5lb to roughly 16lbs. When used correctly, they are easy and damage-free.

o You may need to affix a nail into the wall for heavier objects. If this is the case, you should use a stud finder to locate a support beam, especially if you are hanging items like shelves or mirrors. A stud is a solid wooden beam that runs from the floor to the ceiling so that it will offer you the most support. They often run between 16″ to 24″ apart.

o When nailing into the wall, tap lightly with a hammer, so you don't accidentally hit the wall and create a large hole.

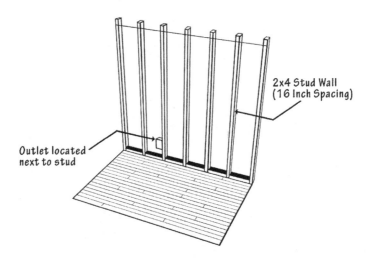

o You can purchase picture hanging kits at most hardware stores which will come with hooks, picture wire, nails, etc.

CAR CARE

1. Filling the Gas Tank

Hopefully, someone has taught you how to fill the gas tank if you know how to drive. With that said, there are many reasons why you might not know how to fill up your tank, and that's okay. If you have yet to learn, here are the basics of filling up.

Gas tanks can be found on either side of the car. There is typically a picture of a gas tank with an arrow indicating which side it is on.

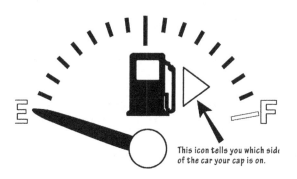

This icon tells you which side of the car your cap is on.

Gas tanks will have a lever on the floor of the driver's side door, a button to unlock the tank door, or will simply pull open. Some older cars have locks and keys to access the gas tank, but that is uncommon.

Once the tank door is open, twist the cap counterclockwise to open. If the gas cap is not attached to the tank by a plastic strip, see if there is a slot to slide it in while you pump gas. Whatever you do, don't lose the cap.

After filling the tank, the pump will click and stop when the tank is full. There can be false stops, so try pumping again if it seems like it stopped too soon.

Once the tank is full, replace the cap by twisting clockwise and close the tank door.

Most gas pumps require a credit card payment at the pump or an in-store purchase with cash. If purchasing with cash, you will have to walk into the store, tell the clerk your pump number and how much money you want to spend on gas. Often this exchange looks something like, "May I get $20 on pump eight, please?" If you fill up for less cash than you paid, walk back in, and the clerk will refund you the difference.

2. Checking the Oil

Knowing how to check the oil yourself is a valuable skill to learn. Most cars have a light that appears when it is time to get an oil change. The check oil light looks like a magic lamp.

You will need to turn off your car and open the hood to check the oil. Most cars have a lever on the driver's side near the door or on the floor. Once you have "popped the hood," you will need to open it and prop it up.

Some hoods have a latch in the center of the hood to prevent it from popping open accidentally while driving. Slide your fingers under the hood and feel for the latch to open.

Once the hood is open, on the side (could be left or right), there will be a long metal rod you need to use to prop the hood open.

Look at the engine, and you will see the oil cap; it should have the same picture on it as the check oil light. Next to it will be the dipstick. Pull out the dipstick and wipe it off with a clean rag, then reinsert it and pull it out once more.

Look at the end of the dipstick; it may have the word "full," or you may notice a change in texture or thickness. The oil should be a light amber color. If the oil is dark and dirty or the level is low, you need to head in for an oil change. If the oil level is ok, reinsert the dipstick and keep driving. If your check oil light continues to come on, you may have a sensor issue or other problem.

3. Tire Pressure

To avoid a flat tire and to keep your car driving safely, your tires need to have the appropriate amount of air pressure in them. When the pressure is low, your vehicle has less traction, which can cause dangerous driving situations.

The dashboard will have a light indicating your tire pressure is low; some modern cars have a digital display that shows the pressure level.

There are handheld devices you can keep in your car to check tire pressure, or you can stop at any gas station that has an air pump; they are usually located off to the side or around the back.

Remove the small cap on your car's wheel to check the tire pressure and place it somewhere safe.

Affix the nozzle of the tire pressure hose or tire pressure device onto the valve and push gently. The device or the air tank will show you a number that will tell you the tire's pressure level.

There is usually a sticker that will tell you the optimal psi (pounds per square inch) for your car's tires on the inside of the driver's side door. Most sedans will fall in the 30-35 range, and most SUVs will be slightly higher, possibly into the 40s. This information should also be in your car's owner's manual.

If your tire pressure is low, you will need to add air. Some gas stations offer free air, but many charge a minimal fee.

Press the nozzle onto the valve and depress the lever to add air. The psi reading will change on the screen as your tire fills with air. Unless your car has a digital display that tells you the psi for all four tires, it is a good idea to check them all simultaneously.

4. Jump-Starting Your Car

If your car battery dies, you will need to jump it to get your car started again. It is a great idea to keep a set of jumper cables in your car just in case. A car battery often dies when the car's exterior or interior lights are left on, or it can happen in extreme cold.

You will need another car or a portable jumpstart device. It is best to read your car's owner manual for specific instructions. Below is a graphic outlining the standard steps.

How to Use Jumper Cables to Jump-Start a Car from Another Vehicle:

Check Batteries: Ensure that the battery giving the jump has enough voltage and matches the voltage system type (12V,6V, etc).

Ready Cars: Put both cars into park or neutral, turn off the ignition, and put on the parking brake.

Open the Hood of each car.

Attach Alligator Clips to the terminals in the following order:

① Red to Dead - Connect the red, or positive, clip to the positive terminal on the donor battery of the dead car.

② Red to Donor - Connect the red, positive clip, to the positive terminal on the donor battery in the other car.

③ Black to Donor - Connect the black clip to the negative terminal of the donor car.

④ Black to Metal - Connect the black clip to an unpainted metal part of the dead car that is not directly next to the battery. One of the metal struts that hold the hood open is a good place to connect the second black, or negative, clip.

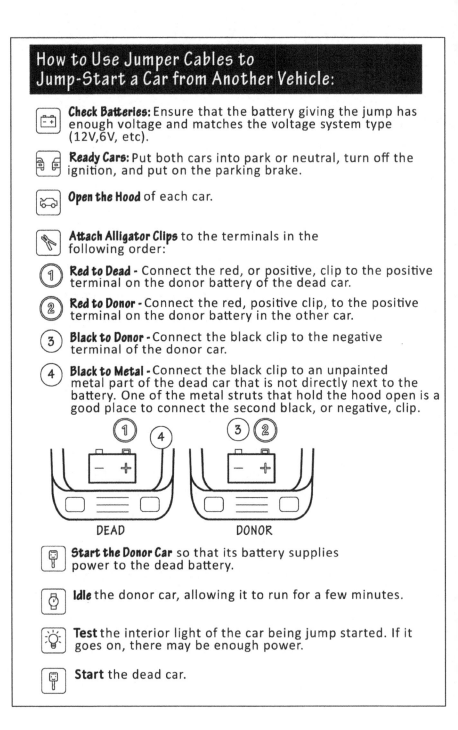

DEAD   DONOR

Start the Donor Car so that its battery supplies power to the dead battery.

Idle the donor car, allowing it to run for a few minutes.

Test the interior light of the car being jump started. If it goes on, there may be enough power.

Start the dead car.

128

MAPS AND DIRECTIONS

1. Reading a Map

With modern GPS devices, many of us have forgotten or never learned how to read a map. Understanding the basics can help you in a pinch if your phone dies or you lose signal.

A map uses four primary directions: North, East, South, and West. If you are holding a map upright, north is the top, south is the bottom, east is the right, and west is the left.

To properly use a map, you will need to know where you are and where you want to go.

A map will have what is called a legend located near one of the corners. The legend is a key to helping you decipher what different objects on the map are.

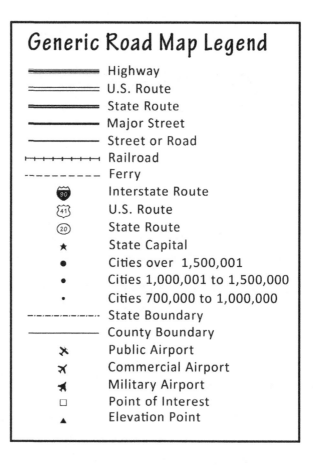

Generic Road Map Legend

=================	Highway
=================	U.S. Route
=================	State Route
───────	Major Street
───────	Street or Road
┼─┼─┼─┼─┼─┼	Railroad
─────────	Ferry
(90)	Interstate Route
(41)	U.S. Route
(20)	State Route
★	State Capital
●	Cities over 1,500,001
●	Cities 1,000,001 to 1,500,000
•	Cities 700,000 to 1,000,000
─·─·─·─·─··	State Boundary
───────	County Boundary
✗	Public Airport
✗	Commercial Airport
✈	Military Airport
□	Point of Interest
▲	Elevation Point

Major roads are usually highlighted in a bright color and drawn with thick lines, so they are easy to see. They will also have the road number listed on them periodically.

2. Traffic Terms

Knowing traffic terms will help you navigate the roadways with or without a map. Here are some basic terms you should know:

- Freeway: an express highway with controlled access.
- Highway: a major road that typically connects major towns and cities, usually has no traffic lights or signals.

- Exit: the exit point off of a freeway or highway onto another road.
- Curves: parts of the road that have been deemed exceptionally curvy and potentially dangerous when driving at accelerated speeds.
- Toll Road: a freeway that requires you to pay a fee to drive on. The fee could be collected as you enter or before you exit the road.
- Speed Limit: The maximum speed you are permitted to drive on that particular road. Some major roads have a minimum speed limit as well.

3. Public Transit Timetable & Map

If you plan to travel by bus or train, understanding how to read a timetable can come in handy.

Each city, town, company, etc., will write its own schedule, but some basic components are fairly universal.

The schedule will show a list of the stops along the line and the arrival times of the bus or train at each point.

The schedule below shows Bus A picking up at the market at 8:00. The bus will arrive at the school at 8:47.

	BUS A	BUS B	BUS C	BUS D
Market	08:00	10:20	12:20	16:55
Cinema	08:10	10:32	12:26	17:10
Hospital	08:25	10:48	12:42	17:33
School	08:47	11:10	13:11	18:01

Some timetables will read up and down like the one above, and others will read left to right. Most bus and train lines will have several routes, so you will need to know where you are, where the closest stop is, and where you need to go.

Typically, the different routes or lines are distinguished by color and a small dot or circle to show where they stop. When the two dots are side by side or overlap, both lines stop at the same location. These are the locations where you can switch trains or buses if needed.

The directional arrows show you which direction the line travels. Many train and subway lines will run in both directions, so you must board the correct one, or you'll be headed in the opposite direction. Usually, the direction it is traveling is indicated by the last stop.

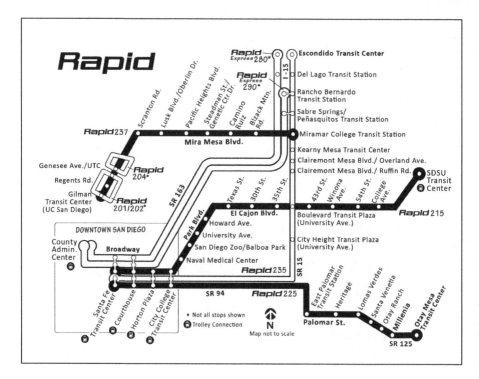

4. Flight Schedules

Traveling by plane is fun and exciting, but it can be stressful if you don't know how to read a flight schedule.

You will need to know what airport you are flying out of and what airport you want to fly into to book a flight. Travel websites will help you with this information if you type in the closest city to where you are. Each airport has a three-letter code; for example, Orlando International Airport is MCO.

The flight schedule will list the airport codes and the departure and arrival time (usually in local time). It will also list if there are any stops or if it's a nonstop flight. It will also state whether you need to transfer planes during that stop.

Longer flights often have one stop along the way to refuel and transfer passengers at major airports. Still, you may not need to switch planes depending on your final destination.

The schedule will also tell you how long the flight is, the flight number, and the price.

New York (JFK), NY to Los Angeles, CA

■ ✈ Air   Total Price: $99.50

ITINERARY

Travel Data	Flight Segments		Flight Summary
DEPART SEP 05 **FRI**	10:30 AM Depart from New York, NY (JFK) on Sunny Airlines	Flight #950	Friday, September 5, 2019
	16:05 AM Arrive in Los Angeles, CA (LAX)	🛜 WiFi available	Travel Time 5h30m (Nonstop) **Wanna Get Away**
RETURN SEP 08 **MON**	08:05 PM Depart from Los Angeles, CA (LAX) on Sunny Airlines	Flight #943	Monday, September 8, 2019
	13:40 PM Arrive in New York, NY (JFK)	🛜 WiFi available	Travel Time 5h30m (Nonstop) **Wanna Get Away**

CONCLUSION

By reading and keeping this handy book on your shelf, you have now become the master of your own independence—no more frantic searches on the internet or midnight phone calls to mom or dad for help. With this guide, you now have the power to be self-reliant!!

With basic life-skill knowledge comes confidence and leadership. You can pass on your know-how to your friends and younger relatives and become a successful mentor. Even when you're not one-hundred percent sure how to accomplish a task, all you have to do is flip to the page you need, and viola, the clearly described and illustrated answer will be there for you.

Over time, the more you practice the life skills presented in this book, the less you will have to refer to it. They will become second nature in time. Think back to when you first learned how to ride a bike, play video games, or build a LEGO set; it probably felt difficult, if not downright daunting. Now, you can do all those things with ease

Remember, no adult has all the answers, even those who like to pretend they do. But as Thomas Jefferson was known for saying, "Knowledge is power."

Of course, there is never anything wrong with asking for help when needed, but stepping out into the world with a boosted confidence in your abilities will certainly help.

Kids often say they can't wait to become grown-ups until they approach their teen years and realize that adulting can be challenging at times. By reading this guide, you've made your journey into adulthood so much easier. You are now armed with dozens of basic life skills that, sadly, many teens are no longer taught or given a chance to experience.

You are now ready to take your life in your hands with a newly found confidence! And remember, when you need a little refresher, this guide will always be there to help.